NITROGEN DEFICIENCY

GW00728817

POTASSIUM DEFICIENCY

PH PROBLEMS

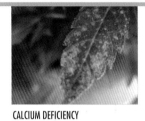

CALCIUM DEFICIENCY

MAGNESIUM DEFICIENCY

PHOSPHOROUS DEFICIENCY

COPPER DEFICIENCY

MOLYBDENUM DEFICIENCY

IRON DEFICIENCY

ALSO INCLUDES BORON, SULFUR & ZINC
DEFICIENCIES

MANGANESE DEFICIENCY

PEST INVASIONS

MEALY BUGS AND MITES

WHITEFLIES

APHIDS

THRIPS

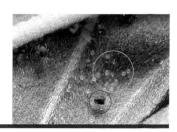

SPIDER MITES

SPIDER MITES

ANTS

CATERPILLARS AND SLUGS

LEAF MINERS

ALSO INCLUDES INFORMATION ON DEER,
FUNGUS GNATS, GOPHERS, MOLES AND RATS

CORN BORERS

PLANT DISEASES

POWDERY MILDEW

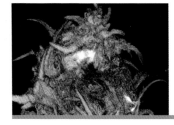

LEAF SEPTORIA

MOLDY BUD

ROOT ROT

FUSARIUM WILT

ENVIRONMENTAL STRESSES

NUTRIENT BURN

LIGHT BURN

OVERWATERING

AND MUCH MORE!

HEAT BURN

MARIJUANA
GARDEN
SAVER

Handbook for Healthy Plants

J. C. STITCH
Edited by ED ROSENTHAL

Marijuana Garden Saver
Handbook for Healthy Plants
Copyright 2008 Quick Trading Company

Published by Quick American
A division of Quick Trading Co.
Oakland, California
ISBN-13: 978-0-932551-91-7

J.C. Stitch
Executive Editor: Ed Rosenthal
Editorial Staff: Emily Peacock, Andrew Glazier, Paul Suliin
Project Manager: Hera Lee
Cover and Interior Design: Hera Lee

Thanks to all the individuals who contributed photographs.
Interior photographs by Ed Rosenthal unless otherwise noted.
Bud photograph on front cover: thanks to Freezerboy.

Printed in China

TABLE OF CONTENTS

INTRODUCTION

INTRODUCTION

Marijuana Garden Saver gives you the tools you need to grow healthy marijuana plants. Section 1 provides information about proper nutrients the plants need and how to identify deficiencies, and includes a guide to pH management. Section 2 covers pests that are most attracted to Cannabis, their effect on the plant, and provides a variety of preventative and problem solving techniques. Section 3 identifies common diseases that can attack marijuana, how they may be prevented and controlled. Section 4 reviews environmental stresses that can impact a garden. Section 5 is a guide to the controls referenced in the preceding sections, with suggested commercial brands.

This book is a troubleshooting guide for people who are growing Cannabis. It is meant to take you over the bumps and help you solve garden problems. Using the information provided here, you will be able to harvest abundant high-quality bud from your garden.

SECTION 1 NUTRIENTS

Nutrient disorders can occur in any growing medium while using any technique—coir, rock wool, soil, soilless, hydroponic or aeroponic. Outdoor growers usually have fewer issues with nutrient disorders than indoor growers, but lack of nutrients can slow growth.

Nutrient problems can be caused by a variety of issues: pH is one huge factor. Nutrient deficiencies make the plants sick. An overabundance of nutrients can result in nutrient burn or toxicity, and can also lock out other ingredients.

In hydroponic systems, the nutrient/water solution should be changed every two weeks because plants use more of some nutrients than others. It's a good idea to rinse at the same time; this helps prevent bacterial or fungal growth that attacks cannabis roots.

All fertilizer packages list three numbers that identify the N-P-K ratio. They usually appear as three numbers with dashes between them such as 25-10-10. The first number represents Nitrogen (N), which is responsible for foliage or leaf development. Fertilizers that promote heavy leaf growth have a higher first number than the other two. The second number is Phosphorus (P), which is important for strong stems and flowering. The third number is Potassium (K), which promotes healthy metabolic function. Sometimes micronutrients are listed after the macronutrients: These are Calcium (Ca), Magnesium (Mg), Copper (Cu), Manganese (Mn), Iron (Fe) and Zinc (Zn).

The ability to absorb nutrients is related to the pH of the water given to the plant. pH is the measurement of how acidic or how basic (alkaline) something is. pH should be viewed like a seesaw. It is important to measure pH after adding nutrients. pH can be adjusted by using commercially available pH-up or pH-down mixtures. Home remedies are available but can cause problems. Commercial products tend to be more concentrated and quite inexpensive. Failing to manage pH levels can cause nutrients to be unavailable and basically wasted. pH is important for soil gardening and so important for hydroponic gardening that failing to monitor pH has disastrous results.

In this section, we list the nutrient deficiencies and how they affect cannabis, in alphabetical order.

We start each nutrient description with a quick reality check: How common is this problem? This is followed by a description of how the plant appears if affected by that particular deficiency. Next is information on its mobility and the role that the nutrient plays in the plant's nutrition. By mobility we mean that once a nutrient is transported to a site and is used to build tissue, can it be moved or is it fixed? Mobile nutrients move to new growth so deficiencies appear on older vegetation. Non-mobile nutrients stay put so that deficiencies appear on new growth. Each nutrient concludes with a guide to fixing the deficiency and getting the plant back to full health.

Unless the damage is slight, individual leaves do not recover from nutrient deficiencies. With non-mobile nutrients, look at new growth to determine whether the deficiency has been solved. With mobile nutrients, especially nitrogen, the damage will be seen first in the older leaves and not in new growth.

pH

pH is a logarithmic measure of the acid-alkaline balance in soil or water. A pH of 1 is the most acidic solution, 7 is neutral and 14 is most alkaline. It has a profound effect on plant growth for several reasons. Different species of plants have adapted to living under different pH levels. Marijuana has been grown in hydroponic solutions with a pH as low as 5.5, but it does best when grown in soil or water within a pH range of 6.0-6.5, slightly acidic. This is the pH of good garden soils. All of the plant nutrients are water soluble in this range so they are readily available to the plants. Outside of this range they become less available.

The only accurate way to adjust the pH is using a pH meter or pH test papers. Guesswork won't do.

When the pH is outside the 6.0-6.5 range the nutrients do not dissolve well and are not as available to the plant. As a result, even though they may be present, plant roots do not have access to them so the plants indicate deficiencies. Plants that are growing in water or soil outside the proper pH range grow very slowly and have small, dark green leaves.

If the plants are to be grown in soil or planting mix, check its pH using a pH meter or test strips before you plant. To do this, used collected runoff water. Adjust the pH using soil sulfur if it is too alkaline or lime if it is too acidic. Check with a knowledgeable local nurseryman or agricultural extension agent familiar with local soils. S/he can give you advice on proportions since soils vary in

pH problems. *Photo: Cemical Burn*

pH problems. *Photo: Cemical Burn*

their reaction to adjustments. Most indoor planting media are not soils at all: they are made using bark, peat moss or coir as a main ingredient and other materials are added to adjust porosity and water retention. These mixes can be considered disease- and pest-free.

Most commercial potting soils and topsoil are already pH balanced.

If the plants are already in the ground and the soil is out of the preferred range, adjust the irrigation water using pH Up to raise alkalinity or pH Down to increase acidity. Recheck the soil pH from time to time to judge when to stop these treatments.

Hydroponic solutions should also be kept in the 6.0-6.5 range using pH-up or pH-down. Strains vary a bit in their ideal pH levels.

Water should be pH adjusted after soluble fertilizers are added to it because their ingredients also affect water pH.

BORON (B)

How common is it?

Boron (B) deficiency is not common. It occurs very occasionally in some western soils.

Symptoms

The first sign of a Boron deficiency is the browning or graying of the growing tips followed by their death. Soon after, the lateral shoots start to grow, but then die. Shoots appear sunburned, twisted and a bright green color. The leaves develop small brown necrotic dead spots that look like strawberry seeds, and are surrounded by an area of dying tissue between leaf veins. Boron deficiency resembles a calcium deficiency, but can be differentiated by the small size of the necrotic areas.

Stems and petioles (leaf stems) are brittle and show signs of hollowness. Boron deficiency only affects newer growth.

Roots become stunted and the smaller secondary roots become short and swollen as the root tips die. The roots are vulnerable to fungal and bacterial attacks that rot the root hairs and cause discoloration.

Boron deficiency. *Photo: Turkish*

Excess boron, which is rare and is caused primarily by over-fertilization, causes the yellowing of the leaf tips which progresses inward. The leaves drop and the plant dies.

Mobility

Boron is not mobile.

Role in plant nutrition

Boron is important in the processes of maturation, pollen germination, and seed production. It also aids in cell division, protein formation, healthy leaf color, and plant structure formation. Proper amounts keep stems, stalks, and branches strong and help plant cells maintain rigidity. It helps calcium maintain soluble.

Problem Solving

Treat a Boron deficiency foliarly or through the irrigation water, using one teaspoon of boric acid (available in drug stores) per gallon of water. Fast-acting solutions also include borax, compost and compost teas.

CALCIUM (CA)

How common is it?

Calcium (Ca) deficiency is rare outdoors except in very acidic soils. The deficiency is occasionally found in planting mixes and is more common in hydroponics. Calcium deficiency sometimes occurs in soil-less growing mediums that have not been supplemented with lime, which is composed mostly of calcium.

Distilled and reverse osmosis water, as well as some tap water, lack significant amounts of dissolved calcium. This can lead to calcium deficiency unless the water is supplemented with calcium.

Symptoms

Calcium (Ca) deficiency stunts plant growth and makes the leaves turn dark green. Large necrotic (dead) blotches of tan, dried tissue appear mostly on new growth but also on other plant parts along leaf edges. Young shoots crinkle and get a yellow or purple color. In severe cases they twist before they die. Necrosis appears along the lateral leaf margins. Problems migrate to the older growth, which browns and dies.

Stems and branches are weak, lack flexibility and crack easily.

The root system does not develop properly, leading to bacterial problems that cause root disease and die-off. The roots discolor to a sickly brown.

Early-stage calcium deficiency. *Photo: Senseless*

Mobility

Calcium is semi-mobile.

Role in plant nutrition

Calcium strengthens plant cell walls and therefore stems, stalks, and branches, and it aids in root growth—mostly the newer root hairs. It travels slowly and tends to concentrate in roots and older growth. Ca also enhances the uptake of K.

Problem Solving

Dolomitic lime, or garden lime, can be added to planting mixes before potting. It provides calcium and also helps stabilize pH over a period of time.

Both planting mediums and hydro systems can be fertilized as directed using a commercial calcium-magnesium formula; this provides instant availability to the plant. It can also be used in planting mixes. Growers often use calcium acetate or calcium-magnesium acetate.

Calcium nitrate ($CaNO_3$) is a water-soluble fertilizer that supplies both calcium and nitrogen. It provides a very soluble form of calcium to the roots and can also be used as a foliar spray. This formula gets calcium to the plant very quickly. Be careful not to add calcium nitrate during the flowering stage because it provides unwanted excess nitrogen.

Calcium deficiency. *Photo: Senseless*

Calcium deficiency. *Photo: Senseless*

There are a number of brands of liquid calcium or liquid lime. These are also quickly absorbed by the roots.

One teaspoon of hydrated lime per gallon of water provides relatively fast absorption. Dolomitic limestone, which contains magnesium and calcium, takes longer to absorb. It is a good ingredient to place in planting mixes to prevent deficiency.

Outdoors, add calcium to acidic soils to bring them into the pH range of 5.9-6.5. Use dolomitic lime, or garden lime. Ground eggshells, fish bones and seashells also break down over the season and add calcium to the soil.

Gypsum, calcium sulfate ($CaSO_4$), can be added to outdoor soils to increase calcium content without affecting the pH too much. It should not be added to soils with a pH below 5.5 because it interacts with Aluminum (Al), making it soluble and poisonous to the plants.

General discussion

Most planting mediums have adequate amounts of calcium. However, calcium should be added to the planting mix if the pH is too low. See pH section for more information.

Hydroponically grown plants are most likely to suffer calcium deficiency. Some hydro fertilizers contain only small amounts of calcium, as the amount of calcium dissolved in the supply water varies. If the water contains more than 150 parts per million (ppm) dissolved solids, it is probably providing the plants with enough calcium. If the water contains less than 150 ppm of dissolved solids, Ca-Mg has to be added to the water. To find out how hard or soft your water is; you will need to have a tds/ppm meter or refer to the local water district quality report.

COPPER (CU)

How common is it?

Copper (Cu) deficiencies are rare.

Symptoms

Copper (Cu) deficiency first appears in young leaves which exhibit necrosis and coppery, bluish or gray with metallic sheen coloring at the tips and margins. The young leaves turn yellow between the veins.

Other symptoms include limp leaves that turn under at the edges and eventually die, and wilting of the whole plant. New growth has difficulty opening, flowers do not mature or open in males and in females the stigmas don't grow properly.

Copper toxicity is rare but fatal. As the plant approaches death, its leaves yellow from its inability to use Iron (Fe). The roots are abnormally sized, then start to decay.

Mobility

Copper has a low mobility.

Though it vaguely resembles nitrogen toxicity, the yellow-white leaf bottoms and brown and dying fan leaf tips confirm the copper deficiency.

Role in plant nutrition

Cu is essential to healthy plant production, reproduction and maturity, and assists in carbohydrate metabolism and oxygen reduction.

Problem Solving

Foliar feeding with copper fungicides such as copper sulfate ($CuSO_4$) and chelated copper adjusts a deficiency. Any hydroponic micronutrient formula containing copper helps as well. Compost, greensand, and kelp concentrates are good natural sources.

Soaking dimes or quarters in water and then using the water to irrigate the plants also supplies copper, since these coins are 92% copper and 8% zinc. (Pennies contain mostly zinc, not copper.) An acid solution dissolves the copper faster.

General discussion

Copper (Cu) deficiencies are often confused with over-fertilization.

IRON (FE)

How common is it?

Iron deficiency occasionally occurs outdoors, in planting mediums, and in hydro.

Symptoms

Iron deficiency starts in the new leaves, which lack chlorophyll but have no necrotic spots. This causes them to turn bright yellow except for the veins, which remain green. New leaves start to experience chlorotic molting; first near the base of the leaflets, so the middle of the leaf appears to have a brown mark. The veins remain dark green. Note that a Fe deficiency looks similar to a Mg deficiency except for its location. Fe deficiency affects the new growth but not the lower leaves while Mg deficiency affects the middle and lower leaves first.

Mobility

Fe moves slowly in the plant.

Iron deficiency. *Photo: Shadow*

Iron deficiency. *Photo: Anonymous*

Role in plant nutrition

Fe is necessary for enzymes to function and acts as a catalyst for the synthesis of chlorophyll. Young actively growing tissues need Fe to thrive.

Problem Solving

An Fe deficiency may indicate a pH imbalance. Foliar feed with Fe chelated fertilizer containing Fe, Zn, and Mn, since these deficiencies are often found in combination. Other Fe-bearing supplements include compost, Fe chelates (often found in hydroponic micronutrient supplements), iron oxides (Fe_2O_3, FeO), and iron sulfate ($FeSO_4$) for fast absorption. Supplements should be added both foliarly and to the planting medium. Adding rusty water also works.

General discussion

An Fe deficiency is often found in combination with Zn and Mn deficiencies.

MAGNESIUM (MG)

How common is it?

Magnesium (Mg) deficiency is common in all mediums and hydro. It is not common outdoors.

Symptoms

Magnesium deficiency starts in the lower leaves. The veins remain green while the rest of the leaf turns yellow, exhibiting chlorosis. The leaves eventually curl up, and then die. The edges of affected leaves feel dry and crispy. As the deficiency continues it moves from lower leaves to the middle to upper half. Eventually the growing shoots change from a pale green to white color. The deficiency is quite apparent in the upper leaves. At the same time, the stems and petioles turn purple.

Mobility

Magnesium is mobile.

Role in plant nutrition

Magnesium helps support healthy veins and maintains leaf production and structure. It's required for chlorophyll production and enzyme breakdowns.

Magnesium deficiency. *Photo: Prawn Connery Of Plant Ganja.com*

Magnesium deficiency apparent in right plant, contrasted with the green healthy plant on left.

Problem Solving

Water-soluble nutrients containing Magnesium fix the deficiency. Such nutrients are magnesium sulfate ($MgSO_4$, Epsom salts) and Ca-Mg for fast absorption; and dolomite lime/garden lime and worm castings for moderate absorption.

In hydro and planting mixes Magnesium deficiencies are easily fixed using 1 teaspoon of Epsom salts per gallon of water in reservoirs or 1 teaspoon per quart of water in planting mixes. After the first treatment, treat with one-quarter dose with each watering or change of reservoir. Calcium-Magnesium can also be used.

For fastest action Epsom salts can be used foliarly at the rate of 1 teaspoon per gallon. Calcium-Magnesium can be used foliarly as directed.

Dolomitic limestone contains large amounts of Magnesium. It can be used to raise the pH of soils and planting mixes and supply Magnesium at the same time.

General discussion

Magnesium deficiency is one of the easiest nutrient deficiencies to diagnose and cure. It occurs more frequently if using distilled, reverse osmosis water and tap water that has low ppm count.

MANGANESE (MN)

How common is it?

Manganese (Mn) deficiency is rare and almost always associated with Fe-Zinc deficiencies.

Symptoms

Manganese deficiency is generally found in the young leaves. The leaf tissues turn yellow and small areas of tan/brown dead tissue (necrotic areas) appear in the middle of the leaf. The leaf veins usually stay green. The leaf becomes outlined in a ring of dark green along its margins. Too much Manganese in the soil causes an Iron (Fe) deficiency. In addition the plant shows a lack of vigor.

Mobility

Manganese is not mobile.

Role in plant nutrition

Mn helps enzymes break down for chlorophyll and photosynthesis production, and it aids in making nitrates available for protein production.

Problem Solving

For fast relief foliar feed with a water-soluble fertilizer high in Mn such as Fe-Zn-Mn fertilizer, hydro micros, or Mn chelate. Then add the fertilizers to the water/nutrient mix. Compost and greensand also contain Mn but they are absorbed more slowly than the water-solubles.

Manganese deficiency. *Photo: Anonymous*

MOLYBDENUM (MO)

How common is it?

Mo deficiency is very rare, but is more likely to occur in color-changing strains in cold temperature conditions.

Symptoms

The middle leaves turn yellow. As the deficiency progresses towards the shoots the new leaves become distorted or twisted. A Mo deficiency causes leaves to have a pale, fringed, and scorched look, along with retarded or strange-looking leaf growth. Older chlorotic leaves experience rolled margins, stunted growth and red tips that move inward toward the middle of the leaves.

Sometimes Mo deficiency is misdiagnosed as a N deficiency. However, N affects the bottom leaves first. Mo affects leaves in the middle of the plant first and then moves up to the newer growth.

Excessive Mo in cannabis looks like Fe or Cu deficiency.

Mobility

Mo is mobile.

Role it plays in plant nutrition

Mo is contained in enzymes that help plants convert nitrates to ammonia, which is required for protein production.

Molybdenum deficiency in late flowering. *Photo: Anonymous*

Problem Solving

Foliar spraying with water-soluble fertilizers aids in overcoming the deficiency. Because plants need molybdenum in such small amounts a hydroponic micronutrient mix is often the most efficient way of supplying it. These fertilizers can be used as foliar sprays or applied to the soil, as well as their customary use in hydroponic nutrient solutions.

General discussion

Generally a Mo deficiency occurs when S and P are deficient. Mo toxicity does not tend to wreak havoc on plants, but excess intake causes severe problems in humans so extra precautions should be taken when using it.

NITROGEN (N)

How common is it?

Nitrogen (N) deficiency is the most commonly occurring nutrient deficiency in cannabis.

Symptoms

Lower leaves first appear pale green. The leaves then yellow and die as the Nitrogen travels to support new growth. Eventually the deficiency travels up the plant until only the new growth is green, leaving the lowest leaves to yellow and wither. Lower leaves die from the leaf tips inward.

Other symptoms include smaller leaves, slow growth and a sparse profile. The stems and petioles turn a red/purple tinge.

Too much nitrogen causes a lush dark green growth that is more susceptible to insects and disease. The stalks become brittle and break from lack of flexibility.

Mobility

Nitrogen can travel anywhere on the plant. Usually deficiency starts on the lower of the plant because nitrogen travels to new growth.

Nitrogen deficiency. *Photo: TheNewGuy*

Nitrogen deficiency. *Photo: TheNewGuy*

Role it plays in plant nutrition

Nitrogen is directly responsible for the production of chlorophyll and amino acids, and it is essential to photosynthesis. It is an essential element of tissue; without it growth quickly stops.

Any water-soluble nitrogen (especially nitrates, NO3) is quickly available to the roots. Insoluble nitrogen (such as urea) needs to be broken down by microbes in the soil before the roots can absorb it. After fertilization, nitrogen-deficient plants absorb N as soon as it is available and start to change from pale to a healthy-looking Kelly green. Deficient plants usually recover in about a week, but the most-affected leaves do not recover.

Nitrogen is the first number of the three number set found on all fertilizer packages, which list N-P-K, always in that order. Any water-soluble fertilizer much higher in N than P and K can be used to solve N deficiencies very quickly. Most hydro "Vegetative Formulas" fall into this category.

Calcium nitrate (CaNO3) is water-soluble and fast acting. It can be used as a foliar fertilizer and in the water/nutrient solution.

Urine, fish emulsion (5-1-1) high-Nitrogen bat or seabird guano also act quickly. In soils high-nitrogen fertilizers such as alfalfa and cottonseed meals, manure, feather meal and fish meal all supply nitrogen fairly quickly but release it over the growing season.

General discussion

Without high amounts of nitrogen, especially during the vegetative growth stage, the plant's yield is greatly reduced. Water uptake slows from vascular breakdown in the plants. N issues happen throughout the entire growth cycle. Plants should never experience an N deficiency during vegetative growth. However, over-fertilizing with N causes problems too.

Tapering off the use of nitrogen towards flowering promotes flowering rather than vegetative growth. However, a small amount of N is always necessary in order for the plant to manufacture amino acids, which use N as an ingredient. This supports flower growth

Nitrogen Deficiency in veg. *Photo: M&M*

Nitrogen deficiency in late flowering. *Photo: BillyBob*

and utilization of P and K. Some "Bloom Boosters" have N-P-K ratios of "0-50-30." While high numbers sound impressive, using this fertilizer too early causes the flowers to be smaller than they could have been. If there is not enough residual N available, the plants are not getting the most out of the fertilizer.

In the middle to the end of the flowering stage, plants frequently show a N deficiency. They're using the nutrients that were stored in the leaves and dropping the their oldest, bottom fan leaves. To prevent the deficiency from getting extreme, switch over to bloom nutrients gradually unless the bloom fertilizer contains some N.

The plants switch to flowering growth over a week. Then they need higher levels of P and K. But they still require N. For this reason during the first week of flowering use 1 part each bloom and vegetative. The second week use 2 parts bloom, 1 part veg. During the third week use 3 parts bloom and one part veg. After that use just bloom formula. Although the plants still need N in flowering, it's not near the amount they need when they are growing vegetatively. By gradually moving from grow nutrients the plants receive enough N to last through the flowering process.

PHOSPHORUS (P)

How common is it?

Phosphorus (P) deficiency is uncommon.

Symptoms

Plants deficient in phosphorus grow slowly and are stunted with small leaves. The older leaves are affected first. First the leaves turn dark green and become weak. The leaves develop dull blue or purple hues. The edges of the leaves turn tan/brown and curl downward as the deficiency works its way inward. Fan leaves turn dark green with a purple or dull blue hue. The lower leaves turn yellow and die.

The stems and petioles turn purple or red. Some strains, however, normally possess red or purple stems and petioles, so these traits are not a surefire sign of phosphorus deficiency.

Plants use high amounts of P during flowering. If they don't get adequate or even abundant supplies, it results in lower yields.

Mobility

Phosphorus is mobile.

Phosphorous deficiency. *Photo: Senseless*

Phosphorous deficiency. *Photo (right): Senseless, (left) MynameStitch*

Role in plant nutrition

Phosphorus aids in root and stem growth, influences the vigor of the plant, and helps seedlings germinate. Phosphorus is extremely important in the reproductive stages and flowering.

Problem Solving

Phosphorus is the second number of the three number ratio listed on fertilizer packages. Water-soluble fertilizers containing high phosphorus fix the deficiency. Bloom fertilizers are high P formulas. High-P guano also provide readily available P. Rock phosphate and greensand are also high in P and gradually release it. The affected leaves do not show recovery, but no additional growth is affected and new growth appears healthy.

General discussion

Deficiency during flowering results in lower yields, but over fertilizing can result in "chemical buds" or burn the plant. Cold weather (below 50° F/10° C) can make phosphorus absorption very troublesome. For this reason soluble P such as found in water soluble bloom formulas can add flower yield in cool weather.

POTASSIUM (K)

How common is it?

Potassium (K) deficiency occurs occasionally in both planting mediums and outdoors in soil, but rarely in hydroponics. Plants often suffer from mild potassium deficiencies, even in rich, well-fertilized soil, usually caused by improper fertilization. Many organic fertilizers such as guano, fish emulsion, alfalfa, cottonseed and blood meals, and many animal manures contain minor amounts of potassium relative to nitrogen and phosphorous.

Symptoms

Plants suffering from minor deficiencies look vigorous, even taller than the rest of the population, but the tips and edges of their bottom leaves die or turn tan/brown and develop necrotic spots.

As the deficiency gets more severe the leaves develop chlorotic spots. Mottled patches of red and yellow appear between the veins, which remain green, accompanied by red stems and petioles. More severe deficiencies result in slower growth, especially when plants are in the vegetative stage. Severe potassium shortages cause leaves to grow smaller than usual.

Larger fan leaves have some dead patches, or necrosis, on their margins. These leaves eventually turn brown and die off. Plants with potassium deficiencies tend to be the tallest.

Potassium deficiency: day 21. *Photo: Senseless*

Potassium deficiency. *Photo: MTF-Sandman*

Excess potassium causes fan leaves to show a light to dark yellow or white color between the veins.

Mobility

Potassium is mobile.

Role in plant nutrition

Potassium is found in the whole plant. It is necessary for all activities having to do with water transportation, as well as all stages of growth; it's especially important in the development of buds. K aids in creating sturdy and thick stems, disease resistance, water respiration, and photosynthesis.

Problem Solving

Although symptoms of minor potassium deficiency affect the cosmetic look of the plant, it does not seem to affect plant growth or yields.

Water-soluble fertilizers containing high potassium fix the deficiency. Bloom fertilizer usually contains high potassium levels. It is used in the formulas to balance the pH. Highly alkaline potassium is used to balance acidic P. Wood ashes deliver K quickly.

Liquefied kelp, bloom fertilizers and wood ash are commonly used and work quickly to correct K deficiencies. So do potassium bicarbonate ($KHCO_3$), potassium sulfate (K_2SO_4) and potassium dihydrogen phosphate (KH_2PO_4). Potassium silicate (K_2SiO_3) can be

Potassium deficiency. *Photo: General Ganja*

used to supply Si and has 3% K in it. Granite dust and greensand take more time to get to the plant and are not usually used to correct deficiencies, but to prevent them.

Damaged leaves never recover, but the plant shows recovery in four to five days with applications of fast-acting products.

General discussion

Cold weather slows K absorption, as does too much Ca or NH_4+. High levels of Na displace K.

SILICON (SI)

How common is it?

Si deficiency is very rare.

Symptoms

A Si deficiency prevents the plant from developing strong leaves, stems or roots. It also makes the plant more susceptible to fungal and bacterial diseases and insect infestation. The plant also exhibits a reduction in its photosynthetic activity and overall yield is reduced.

Mobility

Silicon is not mobile.

Role in plant nutrition

Si helps the plant overcome different stresses that occur and helps to protect the plant from pests and diseases. It aids in growth, development, yield and disease resistance. It is used to strengthen stem and branch structure.

Problem Solving

- Diatomaceous earth
- Silica planting medium
- Silicate salts
- Liquid Silicon

General Discussion

Si is abundant in nature.

SULFUR (S)

How common is it?

S deficiency is rare.

Symptoms

The first signs of S deficiency are yellowing, young leaves. Leaf growth is slow; leaves become brittle and narrower than usual, and are small and mutated. Buds die off at the tops of flowering plants. Overall growth is stunted. Some S deficiencies may show orange and red tints rather than yellowing. In severe cases the veins of the growing shoots turn yellow with dead areas at the base of the leaf where the blades join. The stems become hard, thin and may be woody. They increase in length but not in diameter.

Too much S stunts the plant and leaf size, and the leaves look brown and dead at the tips. An excess of S looks like salt damage: restricted growth and dark color damage. This is also rare.

Mobility

Like Fe, S moves slowly in the plant. Warmer temperatures make S harder for the plant to absorb. But unlike Fe, S is distributed evenly throughout the plant, mainly in the big fan leaves. S deficiency starts at the back of the leaves and creeps towards the middle.

Sulfur deficiency. *Photo: Anonymous*

A sulfur deficiency. Notice how the yellowing is starting at the top back of the leaf and moving toward the front. *Photo: SmknVtec*

Role in plant nutrition

S is essential during vegetative growth and plays an important role in root growth, chlorophyll supply, and plant proteins.

Problem Solving

Both organic soils and inorganic fertilizers contain high levels of available S so plants are not likely to suffer from a lack of the element. However, a deficiency is easily solved using Epsom salts ($MgSO_4$). Water the plant with Epsom salts until the condition improves. Mix one to two teaspoons of the salt per gallon and apply both foliarly and to the irrigation water. Adding nutrients containing S fixes the deficiency. Mix at recommended strength to avoid nutrient burn. Any water-soluble fertilizer that uses sulfur in the trace minerals also works. Other sources are elemental garden sulfur, potassium sulfate (K_2SO_4), and gypsum. Do not use gypsum on acidic soil (pH less than 5.5); it affects the absorption of soil aluminum, which is poisonous to plant roots.

ZINC (ZN)

How common is it?

Zn deficiency occurs occasionally.

Symptoms

New growth has radically twisted leaf blades. Zinc deficiencies are identifiable by spotting, chlorosis, and yellowing between the veins of older leaves. Inter-veinal yellowing is often accompanied by overall paleness. During the flowering stage, buds may contort, twist and turn hard. When the deficiency first appears, the spotting can resemble that of an Fe or Mn deficiency but it affects the new growth.

Zn excess is very rare, but produces wilting and even death in extreme cases.

Mobility

Zn is not mobile in plants, so symptoms occur mainly in the newer growth.

Role it plays in plant nutrition

Zn aids in plant size and maturity, as well as in the production of leaves, stalks, stems, and branches. Zn is an essential component in many enzymes and in the growth hormone, auxin. Low auxin levels cause stunted leaves and shoots. Zinc is also important in the formation and activity of chlorophyll. Plants with high levels of zinc can tolerate longer droughts.

Problem Solving

Use an Fe-Zn-Mn micro mix to solve the deficiency. Zinc sulfate ($ZnSO_4$), chelated Zn or zinc oxide (ZnO) also adjust the deficiency.

General discussion

With low levels of Zn in the plants, the yields are dramatically reduced.

Note: Zn, Fe, and Mn get locked out when the pH is too high. These deficiencies often occur together.

SECTION 2 PESTS

Pests in the garden are among the most annoying and difficult problems. No matter the growing method, pests can infect the garden. Pests travel in on clothes and pets. This is a good reason not to allow animals in the grow room.

Make sure that the planting mix is composed of inert or pasteurized ingredients. Planting mix that is not pasteurized can contain bugs.

The larger an insect infestation the harder it is to eradicate, and greater the chances that it includes pests that are resistant to chemical warfare.

This section provides information that allows you to recognize and eradicate pests that affect Cannabis plants. As with the nutrients, the pests are listed in alphabetical order, but the ones that are most likely to attack Cannabis are: Aphids, Fungus Gnats, Mealy Bugs, Scale, Spider Mites, and Whiteflies. A description of each pest is provided so that you can detect it both from the pest itself and by the damage that is done. Preventative and control methods are provided to both keep the pest away from the plants and get rid of an infestation.

ANTS

How common are they?

Ants are abundant both indoors and outdoors. Most of the species that affect marijuana use it for grazing their herds of aphids and mealy bugs.

What does the pest look like?

Ants are made up of three main body parts: the head, thorax and abdomen. All six legs are attached to the thorax and the eyes, jaw and antennae are connected to the head. Ants are generally quite small, usually only about 0.1 to 0.2 inch (about 2 to 5 mm) long.

Where is the pest found?

Ants can be found in the soil or planting medium, where they nest. They climb the stalk and graze their herds of aphids and mealy bugs on the leaves.

What does it do to the plant?

They make their homes in underground colonies and must burrow to travel, thus causing damage to roots and root hairs. The aphids and mealy bugs they herd are severe threats to plants because they suck vital juices.

General discussion

Ants are attracted to plants that already have aphids, whiteflies, mealy bugs, and scale. Then they take these pests to new grazing areas. First they spread out on the plant, and then move the herd to new plants. They hang out (in moving streams) on the plant and in and around the soil/medium.

Aphids, mealy bugs, and whiteflies secrete a sticky substance known as "honeydew," which consists of a sugar concentrate from the plant's sap. Ants adore this honeydew, but this sticky annoyance also attracts sooty mold. Even if the plants do not have infestations of other pests, it is important to exterminate ants because of their ability to carry pests to the plants.

Reproduction rate and life cycle: Ants are social creatures, living in colonies of queens and supported by workers. Some species have only one queen per colony, while others may have several. The ant life cycle begins with an egg laid by a queen, then progresses

Ants tending aphids.

through a larval stage, pupal stage, and finally to adulthood. In many species only the oldest adults work outside the colony. 90% of the ants work in the nest. Colonies reproduce when a newly hatched queen selects several males and either walks or flies to a new location.

Ants regulate their reproductive rates depending on conditions in the colony and the outside environment. They do this partly by regulating the length of the pupal stage and partly by selecting certain larvae or pupae to be transformed into queens and drones. If weather is suitable and there is ample food and water for the size of the colony they reproduce faster, then slow down when conditions become less favorable. What this means to the gardener is that it is not enough to destroy only the ants you see. You need to eliminate the colony itself because any lost workers are rapidly replaced.

Prevention

There are many ways to deter ants from wandering into the grow area and getting to the plants.

- Moats. Ants don't swim so a moat prevents them from crawling from floor or table to the container. A simple moat can be made using a wide tray and a support such as a thick piece of Styrofoam or a block of wood. Place the plant container on top of the support. Fill the tray with water.

- Make an herbal barrier. Ants are repulsed by cinnamon, cloves and bay leaves. Pour the ground spice in a perimeter around the garden. Ants do not cross. A tea can be brewed from these spices and sprayed on plants to repulse pests.

- Chemical barriers. Boric acid, which is sometimes used as an eye-wash, also can be used as a barrier. Occasionally ants cross this barrier, but they become coated with the powder, which slowly kills them. In addition they carry the poison back to the nest.

- Diatomaceous earth, the skeletons of minute sea animals, is mined and ground into a fine powder. It is often used in swimming pool filters. When used as a barrier and kept dry, it kills insects with its sharp points, which puncture insects crawling over it.

- Sticky paper. Sticky cards or flypaper can be used as a perimeter barrier or the stem could be banded with the stick-um. Don't apply it directly to the stem. Wrap paper around the stem and then apply the sticky substance to the paper. It is an easy non-toxic solution to ants, which works well. Two products that are designed for this are sticky traps and Tanglefoot, which is a stick-um that can be spread on surfaces.

Control

- Spices: Use a cinnamon-clove tea to flush ants from planting mediums. When the dry powder is placed on the soil the ants start vacating the premises. Other natural substances that are repulsive to ants include cayenne pepper, citric extracts, mint extracts, and cream of tartar.

- Boric Acid baits: Ants are interested either in grease and oil or sugars. Most ants that bother plants are sugar lovers. Sweets and fats can be mixed with boric acid to make a toxic ant lunch. See the control section for recipes.

- Pyrethrum: Pyrethrum is a natural plant protector harvested from a chrysanthemum family plant. It is lethal to ants. It is available as powders and sprays.

- Commercial ant baits and stakes use minute amounts of poison to kill ants and carry the toxic substances back to the nest. Many brands are available.

- Carbon dioxide (CO_2)

- Insecticidal Soap

- *Saccharopolyspora spinosa* (beneficial bacteria)

- Water

APHIDS

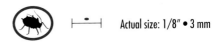

Actual size: 1/8″ • 3 mm

How common are they?

Aphids are a common pest.

What does the pest look like?

Aphids are small pear-shaped soft-bodied insects about 1-3 mm long. There are thousands of species that vary in color from green to yellow, black or brown. Some have wings; some are covered with wax or "wool" made from webbing they secrete, and others have unique distinguishing features.

Common to all aphids, distinguishing them from all other insects, is a pair of "cornicles" extend like tailpipes from their abdomen.

Where is the pest found?

Aphids colonize the stems and undersides of plant leaves. Some species, such as the black bean aphid, are quite noticeable because their color stands out from the plant. Others, such as the green peach orchid, are often colored spring green and blend in with young leaves.

What does it do to the plant?

Aphids live on plant juices by puncturing leaves and sucking sap from stems, branches and leaves. They use a straw-like mouth. In order to obtain enough protein, aphids suck a lot of juice, refine the protein and excrete the concentrated sugar solution that is referred to as "honeydew." This aphid excrement attracts ants that herd the suckers, protecting them from predators. Honeydew is a growth medium for sooty fungus, which causes necrosis of leaf parts.

Heavy aphid infestations cause leaf curl, wilting, stunting of shoot growth, and delay in production of flowers and fruit, as well as a general decline in plant vigor.

Aphids are vectors for hundreds of diseases and can quickly cause an epidemic. They transfer viruses, bacteria and fungi from plant to plant.

General Discussion

Most aphid species have a complex life cycle. They usually overwinter as eggs, but after those eggs hatch most species then produce females that give birth to live young. Indoors they may skip the egg stage entirely, reproducing asexually through live birth year-round. Each live-birth generation takes only 7 to 14 days, and each aphid can produce as many as 100 young, depending on the species. This high reproduction rate lets aphids seem to appear overnight, as a dozen scattered adults can become thousands in just a few days. Indoors, with no predators to keep them in check, they can overrun a garden in short order.

Prevention

Air Filtration: Aphids are airborne for part of their life cycle, so a fine dust filter in the air intake helps to keep aphids out of the grow space.

Monitoring: Check the plants regularly for aphids—at least twice weekly when plants are growing rapidly. Most species of aphids cause the greatest damage when temperatures are warm but not hot (65° to 80°F).

Catch infestations early. Once their numbers are high and they have begun to distort and curl leaves, aphids are hard to control because the curled leaves shelter them from insecticides or natural enemies.

Aphids tend to be most prevalent along the upwind edge of the garden and close to other sources of aphids, so make a special effort to check these areas. Many aphid species prefer the undersides of leaves, so check there.

Outdoors, check for evidence of natural enemies such as lady

Green aphid

Aphids on marijuana leaf

beetles, lacewings, syrphid fly larvae, and the mummified skins of parasitized aphids. Look for disease-killed aphids as well: they may appear off-color, bloated, or flattened. Substantial numbers of any of these natural control factors can mean that the aphid population may be reduced rapidly without the need for treatment.

Control

Sometimes aphids must be controlled outdoors. Often this can be accomplished by spraying them off with water. If they remain a problem consider one of the controls listed in the indoor section. Check for ants: when they are present aphids are much more difficult to control, so they must also be eliminated.

Two different types of aphids—black and green. *Photo: Ed Rosenthal*

Leaves that have been killed by aphids

Indoor Aphid Control

Indoors and in the greenhouse aphids have an easy life. They don't have threats from weather, and since they are in a relatively predator-free area, they don't suffer losses to these relentless killers. Without the pitfalls they suffer in nature, aphid population growth reaches exponential proportions.

Since the balance of nature isn't operative indoors, the gardener must intervene. There are a lot of choices:

Aphid Parasites: Professionals often use parasites when there is an outbreak that hasn't reached epic proportions. Predators are recommended for heavy infestations. However, this may just be a prejudice caused by the subtlety of parasites as compared to the aggressive moves of the predators. The predators spend a portion of their life eating and killing aphids and close-up their actions can be as vicious and dramatic as an alligator's. The parasites just inject an egg into the aphid larvae. The egg hatches and the parasite larvae feasts inside. It emerges as an adult "Alien" style from the mummy. Not quite as dramatic, except when the newborn crawls out of the corpse, but every bit as effective.

Among the most important natural enemies are various species of parasitic wasps (such as *Aphidius matricariae* and *Aphidius ervi*) that lay their eggs inside aphids. The skin of the parasitized aphid turns crusty and golden brown, a form called a mummy. The generation time of most parasites is quite short when the weather is warm, so once mummies begin to appear on the plants, the aphid population is likely to be reduced substantially within a week or two.

Many predators also feed on aphids. The most well known are the common lady beetle (*Hippodamia convergens*), green lacewing (*Chrysopa rufilabris*), and predatory flies (*Aphidoletes aphidimyza*). Naturally occurring predators work best, especially in a small backyard situation. Commercially available lady beetles may give some temporary control when properly handled, although most of them disperse away from the yard within a few days.

Aphids are very susceptible to fungal diseases when it is humid. Whole colonies of aphids can be killed by these pathogens when conditions are right. Look for dead aphids that have turned reddish or brown; they have a fuzzy, shriveled texture unlike the shiny, bloated, tan-colored mummies that form when aphids are parasitized. Make a pesticide by taking these dead aphids, blending them with water (1-3 teaspoons of aphids per quart), and spraying the solution on plants.

- *Beauveria bassiana* (beneficial fungi)
- Capsaicin
- Carbon Dioxide
- Cinnamon oil
- Cloves
- Coriander oil
- Garlic
- Horticultural Oil
- Insecticidal soap
- Neem oil
- Pyrethrum
- Soap
- Vacuuming
- Water Spray

CATERPILLARS (CUTWORMS, CABBAGE WORMS, LEAF-EATERS, CORN BORERS)

How common is it?

In spring and summer caterpillars are common outdoors, but rare indoors.

What does the pest look like?

Caterpillars are the larval stage of butterflies and moths. They have soft, segmented bodies with a head, thorax and abdomen. The thorax contains three pairs of jointed legs that have hooks and the abdomen has five pairs of stumpy legs. Caterpillars are often the same color as the leaves so they are hard to spot. In addition to this general outline, here are some specifics on the types of caterpillars that commonly infest Cannabis:

Cutworms: The adults are gray to dark brown moths with wingspans of 1.25 to 1.75 inch (3 to 4.5 cm). The caterpillars grow to 1 to 1.5 inch (2.5 to 3.75 cm) long, plump and sturdy, ranging in color from brown to pink, green, gray and black. Eggs vary widely by species but are usually laid on the stems or the upper sides of leaves.

Cabbage worms: Also called cabbage loopers. The adults are gray-brown moths with a wingspan of about 1.5 inch (4 cm). The caterpillars are green, usually with narrow white stripes along the body, and may grow up to 1.5 inch (3.75 cm) long. A distinctive feature of the cabbage worm is the way it moves: arching its back to bring its hind legs forward, then extending its body. Eggs are ridged and dome-shaped and usually laid singly on the undersides of leaves.

Leaf-eaters: Many different species. The adults are usually moths, varying widely in color and with wingspans ranging from 1 to 1.75 inch (3 to 4.5 cm). The caterpillars are usually green, but range from gray to brown, and up to 1.5 inch (3.75 cm) long. Some leaf-eaters are "woolybear" caterpillars, their bodies covered with long hairs that look much like fur. The eggs may be found anywhere on the plant, depending on the species.

Corn Borers: The adults are yellow or tan-colored nocturnal moths with wingspans of about 1 inch (2.5 cm). The caterpillars are about 1 inch long, light brown in color with a brown head and spots on each segment. Eggs are white to pale yellow in color, laid in clusters of 20 to 30 on the undersides of leaves.

Caterpillar on cannabis leaf. *Photo: Digital Hippy*

Where the pest is found

Some caterpillars eat leaves. Others bore into the stem and eat the pith, the stem's soft inner tissue. Cutworms feed at night, and spend the day in shallow burrows near the plants.

What does it do to the plant?

Caterpillars eat both leaves and the soft stems. Borers pierce the stem and eat the soft inner tissue. The branches and leaves above the caterpillar wilt, since they receive no water or nutrients. If it is a main stem the whole plant dies. If it is a side stem, only that branch succumbs. In addition to the direct damage they cause, caterpillars leave behind damaged tissues that are more vulnerable to infections.

How they work

Caterpillars are voracious eating machines and can savage plants very quickly. They chew continuously to support their high growth rate. Caterpillars can destroy a tray of seedlings overnight.

General discussion

There are hundreds of species of caterpillar that attack Cannabis. They vary widely in size, color, lifestyle and feeding habits.

Corn borer damage on plant stem. *Photo: Anonymous*

You'll know leaf-eaters and cabbage worms by the large holes that they leave in the plants' leaves. The size of the holes indicates caterpillar damage and not that of smaller pests. Cabbage worms also infest buds: a bud that turns brown and wilts may house a cabbage worm consuming it from within.

Cutworms are perhaps the most obvious of all caterpillars: Plants damaged by cutworms are literally chewed through at the soil line, causing the plant to topple. Seedlings and young plants are completely consumed.

Corn borers attack mature plants - they need a stem large enough to hold their bodies. They lay eggs in clusters on the leaves. After hatching, they eat the leaves around the eggs for two weeks to a month, leaving close clusters of tiny holes. To catch borers early, look for these small holes. Later in the season look for small holes in the plant stalks, possibly covered with thin silky webbing. After borers have been at work for a while they sometimes cause the stalk to develop "fusiform galls." These are bulges in the plants' stalks that widen in the middle and taper at both ends. The borers may leave visible trails on the stalks leading to the galls.

Reproduction rate and life cycle: the moths that give rise to caterpillars generally lay one to two batches of eggs each year, though some species may produce up to six generations per year in warm climates. Each female may lay several hundred eggs. Depending on the species, the adults mate in spring to early summer, and the caterpillars emerge in the early summer to fall. The caterpillars feed until they are ready to enter the pupal stage, when they spin cocoons or dig burrows and hibernate until they emerge as adult moths. Those species that emerge in late summer and fall often overwinter as caterpillars, emerging in early spring to begin feeding again (this is especially common with cutworm species).

In general caterpillars reproduce slowly compared to many pests, but they have large appetites and each one can cause a lot of damage.

Prevention

Because caterpillars vary so widely in their habits, the prevention methods vary widely as well. Planting indoors all but eliminates caterpillars. If you do plant outdoors, keep seedlings indoors as long as possible before transplanting, to prevent caterpillars from wiping them out. Clear the garden of weeds, grasses, and plant debris throughout the year, but especially at the end of the growing season. Use electric "bug zappers" with blue or ultraviolet light to attract and destroy nocturnal moths.

Garlic: repels egg-laying moths.

Cutworms: Plant seedlings as large as possible. Turn the soil two weeks before planting and destroy any larvae you find. Put a "cutworm barrier" around each seedling. An easy one is a metal can with the top and bottom removed, placed around the seedling so it goes at least 1 inch (2.5 cm) into the soil and 4 inches (10 cm) above the soil.

Cabbage worms: Use row covers in spring, when the adult moths breed, to prevent them from laying eggs on the plants.

Caterpillar damage. *Photo: Digital Hippy*

Leaf-eaters: As with cabbage worms, use row covers to block egg-laying adults. Wrap stems with aluminum foil above and below major branches and apply a layer of Tanglefoot or similar stick-um to the foil. These barriers block caterpillars moving along the stems. Turn the soil before planting, especially in the spring, and destroy overwintering larvae and pupae.

Corn Borers: Destroy stalks and other plant debris after harvest.

Control

Quite a few nontoxic and least-toxic methods can be used to eliminate caterpillars.

- If you have only a few plants the easiest way to control caterpillars is physically destroying them. If you spot cutworm damage then you can usually find the caterpillars within about 10 inches (25 cm) of the damaged plants. Raking the soil down to about 2 inches (5 cm) often uncovers them. Other caterpillars can be shaken off plants or handpicked. A spray of water from a hose washes away and drowns caterpillars, and a vacuum cleaner can remove them as well.

- BTK or BT is a living bacterium, *Bacillus thuringiensis*, which the caterpillars ingest. These bacteria sicken caterpillars and certain other pests but are harmless to humans and pets. Once the caterpillars ingest the germ they stop eating and die within a short time. When they die they release new generations of bacteria that are hungry for caterpillar. The insecticide should be used at the first sign of caterpillars.

Caterpillar and/or slug damage. *Photo: Anonymous*

- Cinnamon

- Insecticidal soaps

- Neem oil: Diluted neem oil can be sprayed on plants every 10 days. It makes them unappetizing to caterpillars. Direct hits can be toxic to the leaf-eaters.

- Pyrethrum combined with rotenone

- Soap

- Spinosad: Spinosad's active ingredient is derived from a soil-dwelling bacterium, *Saccharopolyspora spinosa*. The bacterium produces a variety of insecticidal compounds when cultured in fermentation tanks. Spinosad must be ingested, so it has no effect on sucking insects and predators but is deadly to chewers such as caterpillars. Once they ingest the substance insects sicken and die. It is nontoxic to wildlife, pets, and humans with minimal impact on the plants. However use Spinosad with caution around honeybees.

- Trichogramma: Several species of tiny stingless wasps that attack and destroy caterpillar eggs before they hatch. They must be released at the earliest sign of infestation, and cannot be used with most insecticides (BT and Spinosad are exceptions). Consult the supplier for recommended species and coverage rates.

Special note on stem borers: If you do not control stem borers quickly, your yield will be greatly decreased or even non-existent. Before they bore into the stalk they can be eliminated using the same techniques as for caterpillars.

It is a different story once they are situated in the stem's enclosure. Sometimes you can yank the borers right out of the holes they've chewed. Another method is to bore a hole in the stem above the borer and inject one of the recommended caterpillar insecticides into the stem using either a syringe or an eyedropper.

DEER

How common is it?

Deer populations vary widely, both geographically and by habitat. Deer favor light forest and grasslands near forested areas, as they dislike getting more than a few hundred yards from cover. Gardens in suburban areas built near suitable forestland may have problems with grazing deer. Garden plots set up in wild or rural areas are very likely to be visited by deer if the habitat supports them.

What does the pest look like?

Deer are grazers with graceful bodies, thin legs, and long necks. They vary greatly in size depending on species, age, and sex, but usually fall between 4 feet and 6 feet (1.2 and 1.8 meters) long and weigh 80 to 220 lbs (35 to 100 kg). The males carry antlers beginning in late summer, shedding them usually in very late winter through spring.

Where the pest is found

Deer emerge from forest cover at night to browse on plants, but flee quickly when approached. They have excellent senses so most of the time the gardener knows them only by their tracks and the damage they leave.

What it does to the plant

Deer prefer fresh leaves, fruit, and other rich plant matter. In the marijuana garden they strip plants of leaves and buds and even tear up small plants and eat them whole

General discussion

Marijuana evolved cannabinoids in part as protection against herbivores. Most mammals find the leaves and flowers unpleasant. Deer are among the few exceptions. This means that in areas that have large deer populations they may be attracted to your garden simply because it's a food supply that most other herbivores leave alone. Even so they prefer young, tender plants. As marijuana plants mature and cannabinoid levels increase the plants become less palatable for deer.

Deer damage is fairly easy to spot. Since they lack upper incisor teeth they do not bite plants the way a rabbit or similar animal might. Instead the deer takes hold of leaves with its lips and lower teeth, then tears them off. This makes for ragged browse damage, very different from the neatly clipped leaves left by rodents. Look also for deer tracks and droppings near the garden.

Reproduction rate and life cycle: Deer follow a normal mammalian life cycle. Adults mate in the late fall through mid-winter, and the female gives birth to one or sometimes two fawns in late spring to early summer. Deer usually mature in one to two years, and live for 10-20 years if not killed by predators or disease.

Prevention

Naturally deer pose little threat to plants grown indoors. Any outdoor garden near a deer habitat is vulnerable however.

The only effective option to prevent deer damage is to keep them away from the plants. There are two main ways of doing this: repellents and fences. Repellents are less expensive, and may be the only option if discretion is important. But fencing is more certain when it is practical.

Deer find the odors of garlic, capsaicin, and rotten eggs offensive, and commercial repellents containing these ingredients are available under several brands. Other materials also repel deer by smell:

- Anything that carries a human's scent, such as worn clothing or human urine.

- Urine or scat from dogs or other predators. Predator urine is available commercially. Scat is sometimes available from your local zoo.

- Scented bar soap, suspended in a net bag near the plants.

If you are not certain that a repellent is safe for use on food plants then surround the marijuana plants with other plants that you don't plan to eat. Replace the repellent according the manufacturer's instructions, or every few days for the other scent repellents listed above.

Scent isn't the only way to repel deer. Anything that startles or frightens them is effective. Buy several home motion detectors at a hardware store and set them up in a perimeter around the grow site. Depending on the resources at the site motion detectors can be rigged to trigger high-pressure water sprinklers (these are sold as "scarecrow sprinklers"), bright lights, battery-powered radios or ultrasonic noise when a deer approaches. Remember to set up lights to point away from the plants, and if discretion is important then shield the lights or lower the radio volume so the deer can detect them but nearby watchers cannot.

A final word about repellents: Deer can become accustomed to most sounds, sights, or smells. Once they realize that the repellent isn't harming them they'll learn to ignore it. This means that you need to change your repellent from time to time, and not just from one brand to another, but from one ingredient or method to another. Combining methods is also useful. For example, setting up an odor repellent and a scarecrow sprinkler together.

Fencing must be constructed with the abilities and habits of deer in mind. A deer can jump any fence less than 8 feet (2.4 meters) high, if it can get close enough. Fences must also be built tight to the ground, or deer can slip under them. One alternative to an 8-foot fence is an electrified fence. Deer prefer to slip through a barrier rather than jump over it if that looks possible. So a standard electric fence built from 2 or 3 strands of 20-gauge smooth wire on insulated posts often deters them. Once they try to slip between the strands and get shocked they generally keep several feet away from the fence - too far for them to jump it. A variant called a "Minnesota fence" actually uses an attractive bait such as peanut butter to get the deer to lick the fence or a foil tag attached to the fence. The deer gets a mild shock and avoids the fence completely after that.

Control

There is no practical means of controlling deer, in the sense of eradicating them, and this would not be a good option even if there were such a means. The outdoor marijuana gardener should leave the deer's natural predators (mainly coyotes and wild dogs) alone, as these provide some check on the deer population. However aside from that prevention is your best choice.

FUNGUS GNATS

  Actual size: 1/8" • 3 mm

How common are they?

Fungus gnats are common indoors. They are found outdoors occasionally in moist warm areas.

What does the pest look like?

Fungus gnats are 3-4 mm in size, dark grayish black in color and have a slender build with delicate long legs and long wings. The larvae are clear to creamy-white in color with a shiny black head and can be up to .25 inch (6 mm) long.

Where the pest is found

Adults fly close to the soil level and through the plant lower canopy. Fungus gnat larvae live at the root level, usually from 1 to 3 inches (2.5 to 7.5 cm) below the soil line. In shallow containers the larvae may be found wiggling in the drain tray after watering.

What it does to the plant

Fungus gnats' larvae eat roots, root hairs and organic matter, which weakens the plant. They are also vectors for disease. Adult gnats do not eat. They live only to reproduce.

General discussion

Outdoors, adults and larvae live in moist, shady areas. The adults hover near the soil surface. The larvae live at the root level. Fungus

Fungus gnat. *Photo: Anonymous*

Gnat runoff in water. *Photo: 01flat*

gnat larvae attack plant roots growing in planting medium, rock wool and other planting mediums.

Reproduction rate and life cycle: The adult females lay eggs at the surface of moist soil, near the plant stem. The larvae hatch out in four to ten days, depending on temperature, and feed off fungus and plant matter (including plant roots), then pupate in the soil and emerge as adults. The total time from egg to reproductive adult is about four weeks, and each female may lay several hundred eggs in small batches. Indoors, they breed continuously throughout the year and reproduce very rapidly.

Prevention

If plants are outdoors, check the soil for adult gnats or larvae before bringing them indoors.

Prevent indoor entry of gnats by keeping screens on all open windows. Place a barrier over the soil so the gnats have no place to lay their eggs. A piece of cloth, cardboard or a layer of sand all work.

Fungus gnats need moist soil near the surface to reproduce. Let the soil dry between watering as much as the plants will tolerate (usually to a depth of about 1 inch (2-3 cm)). A layer of light, well-draining soil such as vermiculite, perlite, or diatomaceous earth at the top will help with this. This disrupts the larval gnats' food supply and makes it difficult for an infestation to take hold.

Control

- *Bacillus thuringiensis* (beneficial bacteria)
- Barriers (sand, cloth, cardboard, etc.)
- Cinnamon oil and tea
- Diatomaceous earth
- Horticultural oil
- Insecticidal soaps
- Neem oil
- Predatory mites (*Hypoaspis* species)
- Predatory nematodes
  (*Heterorhabditis* and *Steinernema* species)
- Pyrethrum
- Media topping—vermiculite, perlite, diatomaceous earth

GOPHERS

How common are they?

Gophers are a very occasional problem in the garden. They are found mainly in the central and western United States, in Florida, and in Mexico.

What does the pest look like?

Gophers are medium-sized rodents ranging from about 5 to nearly 14 inches (13 to 36 cm) long (not including tail). Their fur is very fine and ranges in color from nearly black to pale brown. The fore-paws have strong claws. The head is small and flattened, with small ears and eyes and very prominent incisor teeth.

Where the pest is found

Gophers tunnel underneath gardens and lawns.

What it does to the plant

Gophers feed on plants in three ways: 1) they feed on roots that they encounter when digging their tunnels; 2) they may venture short distances (only a body length or so) from their tunnels to eat vegetation on the surface; and 3) they pull vegetation into their tunnels from below. Gophers may also attract badgers (which eat them), and the badgers may cause considerable damage when digging for their food.

General discussion

When gophers are suspected the first task is to make sure that they aren't moles instead. Moles cause little direct damage to gardens, and as a result they're seldom worth the trouble to eradicate. It is rare to see either one on the surface, so the best ways to distinguish them are the signs they leave behind.

First, check their diggings: a molehill tends to be a rough cone with a hole or an earthen "plug" near the center. A gopher mound is more fan-shaped, with the hole or plug near one edge. Next, look for damage. Moles generally cause very little damage. Gophers may chew the plants' roots, causing them to wilt and making it possible to pull them up with just a slight tug. If plants are chewed off completely at the soil line, or completely gone, roots and all, then chances are good that there is a gopher problem.

Reproduction rate and life cycle: Gophers mate once a year, in the spring, and produce a litter of up to five young in late spring to early summer. They live for up to 12 years.

Prevention

Containers, indoor gardening, and hydroponic systems offer complete protection against gophers. In field cultivation, minimize weeds, as they are likely to attract gophers. If you are planting directly in the soil, line the planting hole on the bottom and sides with hardware cloth. A border of oleander plants around your garden is reported to repel gophers, but the evidence for this is mainly anecdotal. Any of several commercial gopher repellents (most include castor oil, garlic, or capsaicin) placed in the mouth of the mound may drive them off.

Control

In general, it is best to try repellents first, as they are by far the easiest way to deal with gophers. However sometimes the only solution is to eliminate them.

The simplest means of exterminating gophers is fumigation. Commercial fumigants are generally paper or cardboard cartridges filled with charcoal and potassium nitrate. They're ignited and dropped into the tunnel openings, and the gasses they produce as they burn kill the gophers. Watch for wisps of smoke rising from the ground - these may mark other exits from the gopher's tunnel. Either seal such exits with packed earth or heavy rocks, or kill the fleeing gopher with a shovel as it emerges.

Another possibility for fumigation is carbon dioxide (CO_2). The simplest ways of getting it into the gopher's tunnel are either direct from a CO_2 tank (place the delivery hose in the tunnel opening) or as dry ice. Drop 8 to 16 ounces (225 to 450 grams) of dry ice into the tunnel, or deliver a similar amount of CO_2 from the tank.

Fumigation is not always effective. If not, then trapping is the only way. Suitable traps are available at garden shops, both box traps and lethal forms.

LEAF MINERS

Larvae

Adult

Adult: 1/12" • 2 mm

How common is it?

Leaf miners are not common in indoor marijuana gardens. Outdoors leaves are occasionally attacked, but they are not usually a threat to the plant or yield.

What does the pest look like?

Leaf miners in Cannabis are usually the larval form of various species of flies, though a few species of moths and beetles also produce leaf-mining larvae. These larvae are very small maggots - seldom more than 3 mm long - ranging in color from white to pale green. The adult flies resemble tiny houseflies, about 2 mm long.

Where the pest is found

Leaf miners are found in the leaves, under the surface and in the tissue.

What it does to the plant

The leaves look like someone carved scribble lines into them. These little creatures are a pain to get rid of. While the miners eat and dig squiggly lines into your leaves, they plant their eggs deep inside, and they keep multiplying. When they hatch, the larvae feed off of your leaves until they get big enough to pupate. Pupation occurs within the leaf or in the soil beneath the plant. Once they emerge they repeat this cycle and cause a bigger infestation.

Leaf miners leave the plants open to pathogens and fungi. Leaf damage causes low yields. When the females dig to lay eggs, plants secrete a sap that attracts ants and flies, thus inviting more infestations and problems.

How it works

Leaf miners eat their way through leaves.

General discussion

There are many different varieties of leaf miners, and an expert can distinguish between species by the characteristic appearance of the tunnels. They have evolved their unique form of attack as a means of avoiding the THC and other insecticidal substances on the surfaces of the leaves.

Reproduction rate and life cycle: Female leaf miners implant eggs in leaves - one at a time but often in close batches. Females may lay up to 350 eggs each, depending on species. Eggs hatch in two to six days, and larvae begin tunneling. Eventually they become pupae (either dropping to the ground or remaining in the leaf, depending on species). The pupae develop into adults and the cycle repeats. Expect two to six generations per year outdoors, but indoors a single generation can take as little as a month, and they reproduce year-round.

Prevention

Outdoors, other plants such as lambsquarter, columbine, or velvetleaf can be planted near Cannabis to deter the leaf miners.

Control

If only a few leaves are affected, remove and discard them. Naturally occurring parasitic wasps usually help control the population.

- *Beauveria bassiana* (beneficial fungi)
- Capsaicin
- Horticultural oil
- Neem oil
- Parasitoid Wasps
- Pyrethrum
- *Saccharopolyspora spinosa* (beneficial bacteria)

Leaf miner damage. *Photo: Digital Hippy*

MEALYBUGS
AND SCALE

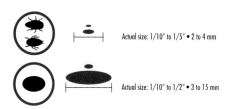

Actual size: 1/10″ to 1/5″ • 2 to 4 mm

Actual size: 1/10″ to 1/2″ • 3 to 15 mm

How common are they?

Mealybugs and scale occasionally attack Cannabis.

What does the pest look like?

These pests are closely related to one another, but take their names from their appearance. Mealybugs are named for the white, "mealy" wax that covers their bodies. On plants they look like tiny puffs of cotton, usually in crevices joints between branches. The adult female insects beneath the wax are 0.1 to 0.2 inch (2-4 mm) long, with flat, oval, segmented bodies. Males are tiny flies that do not have the females' waxy covers.

Scales are so-called because the adult females produce hard shells that resemble tiny "scales" or bumps on the stems and leaves of the plants. Scales vary widely within this general model: from round to oval in shape, from white to dark brown in color, and from 0.1 to 0.5 inch (3 to 15 mm) in diameter. As with mealybugs, adult male scales resemble tiny flies.

Mealy bugs and mites on leaf underside. *Photo: Ed Rosenthal*

Scale. *Photo: Medved*

Where the pest is found

Mealybugs plunk themselves at the nodes. Scales are found on leaf surfaces (especially the undersides), on stems and in crevices. Occasionally scales or mealybugs colonize the stem right at the soil level, where the stem joins the roots.

What it does to the plant

Female scales and mealybugs feed on plant sap. The males, on the other hand, are short-lived as they do not feed at all as adults and live only to fertilize the females. Some species have developed a symbiotic relationship with ants similar to that of aphids. Ants protect and herd them to collect the "honeydew", concentrated sugars that they exude as waste. If there are no ants to eat it, it's quickly colonized by sooty mold. The plant is weakened by the insects' leech like action on their vital juices and the honeydew droppings create mold infections on the stems and leaves. Scales and mealybugs often carry diseases that infect the plants.

General Discussion

Mealy bugs are considered a specialized scale. Both are in the same order as aphids and whiteflies, and are true bugs in the biological sense. Like all true bugs they have specialized probing and sucking mouthparts that they use to drain plant juices.

Female scales and mealybugs tend not to move much as adults. They attach themselves to the plant and produce a protective layer to ward off predators while they suck the plant juices. Mealybugs cover themselves with a web of cottony wax that some potential predators avoid. Scales produce hard shells that armor them against their enemies.

Reproduction rate and life cycle: The overall life cycle is the same for both mealybugs and scales. The females produce 200 to 1000 tiny eggs that they shelter either on or beneath their bodies. When the eggs hatch (in 1 to 4 weeks) the very small (less than 1 mm) nymphs spread out over the plant and begin to feed. In a few weeks they develop into either winged males or stationary, shelled females. The entire generation takes 1 to 2 months, and depending on the species they produce anywhere from one to six generations in a year.

Control

Mealybugs are relatively easy to eliminate on marijuana plants because the plant's structure does not offer easy places for them to hide and protect themselves.

Hand-wipe with sponge or Q-Tip: Mealybugs tend to locate in plant crevices and other hard to get to spots. A Q-tip moistened with isopropyl alcohol is an ideal tool for reaching them.

- Alcohol Spray
- Limonene products kill mealybugs and scale on contact.

Scale. *Photo: Medved*

- Herbal sprays containing cinnamon, clove or other insect repellant herbal oils are very effective exterminants. They kill both on contact and by their evaporates, especially in the protected areas mealybugs choose as habitats.

- Pyrethrum

- Neem oil

- Parasitoid wasps that are specific to various species of mealybugs and scale are available. Some wasp species include *Leptomastix dactylopii*, *Anagyrus pseudcocci*, and *Metaphycus helvolus*.

- Mealybug destroyer: *Cryptolaemus montouzieri* is a ladybug that preys on many species of mealybugs

- The minute pirate bug (*Orius* species) eats mealybugs and scale among other pests.

- The lady beetle *Ryzobius lophanthae* is a voracious soft scale predator. It is opportunistic and also eats aphids and mealybugs when it encounters them. However, it is most effective on scale.

- Horticultural Oil, especially sesame oil products.

- Insecticidal Soaps

MOLES

How common are they?

Moles are common in temperate rural areas, less so in cities and suburbs. They may gravitate to outdoor hemp fields because cultivation loosens the soil and makes it more hospitable to the insects that moles eat.

What does the pest look like?

Moles are burrowing mammals about 5 to 7 inches long, weighing 3 to 4 ounces. They have soft dark fur, very small eyes, pointed snouts, and strong digging claws on their front feet. Moles seldom appear on the surface, though. The gardener usually notices their burrows instead.

Where the pest is found

Moles build tunnel complexes in rich soil. They eat insects and earthworms, and therefore favor moist soils with a lot of soil-dwelling insect life.

What it does to the plant

Moles seldom damage plants directly. However their tunnels and mounds may allow plant roots to become dry, or create a hazard for careless walkers.

General discussion

Generally the most important consideration in dealing with moles is distinguishing them from gophers, which can be much more destructive. The marijuana farmer has little to worry about from moles - once he is sure they are moles. The clearest distinction between them is the shape of their diggings: a molehill tends to be a rough cone with a hole or an earthen "plug" near the center. A gopher mound is more fan-shaped, with the hole or plug near the narrow end.

Reproduction rate and life cycle: Moles generally have one litter of two to five pups per year, in mid to late spring. Except for the spring breeding period they tend to be solitary and highly territorial. They fight other moles even to the death if one invades another's tunnel system.

Prevention

If you are planting directly in the soil, line the planting hole on the bottom and sides with hardware cloth. Repellents may work in outdoor gardens. A number of manufacturers sell devices that they claim repel moles by sending irritating vibrations through the soil. However the evidence for these claims is mostly anecdotal. Odor repellents such as predator urine may be more effective, but the best-attested repellent is castor oil, sold in various brand-name formulations.

Controls

If moles aren't causing root damage then there is really no need to get rid of them. However if it is necessary to rid the garden of moles then the methods are the same as for gophers: fumigation or trapping. The commercial fumigant cartridges sold for gophers also work against moles, as does carbon dioxide from dry ice or a tank. Garden supply shops sell many kinds of mole traps, both the live-trap and lethal kind.

RATS

How common are they?

Rats are not common pests in marijuana gardens, but may sometimes kill plants by gnawing or digging. They are a very environment-specific problem, as they view Cannabis as a target of opportunity.

What does the pest look like?

Rats are rodents ranging from 10 to 16 inches (25 to 40 cm) in length, not including their long tails. They weigh 6 to 12 ounces (170 to 340 grams), and have dark fur ranging from brown to black. Their heads are long and taper to a snout with long whiskers, and their ears are rounded and prominent.

Where the pest is found

Rats are common wherever humans live, although they are not always visible. Some rats live in the wild, feasting on insects, other small animals, nuts, fruits, and nature's detritus. They lair in burrows, walls, piles of trash, dense brush, attics - wherever they can build a secure nest.

What it does to the plant

Marijuana is not a primary food source for rats. In fact, they may not eat it at all. Instead rats like to chew the woody stalks of plants. This cuts the plants down, and the rats usually simply leave it at that, not eating the rest of the plant. A rat's teeth grow constantly throughout its life, and this gnawing behavior is instinctive to keep them from getting too long. Cannabis is like chewing gum for rats.

General discussion

Rats do not go looking for marijuana plants; they go after them only if they're convenient. This means that rats are a problem for the marijuana garden only when the grow site is close to something that they do like to eat. Gardens are at risk for damage by rats near cornfields, orchards, food warehouses, areas with nuts or berries growing wild, and similar places. Food at campsites draws rats close to the garden, so secure all food and destroy or remove all food scraps.

Reproduction and life cycle: Rats are prolific breeders. They can breed year-round if they have a warm place to keep their young, and each female can produce four to nine litters a year (of which anywhere from 12 to 60 young live to adulthood). They adjust their population automatically to the local food supply.

Prevention

An ounce of prevention is worth many pounds of cure with rats. Rats do their damage in a matter of minutes, and a single rat can destroy several plants in one night. By the time you know you have a rat problem it is often too late. Humans have been fighting rats for thousands of years, and if numbers are any guide then the rats are at least holding their own.

If at all possible, minimize the amount of tasty rat-food in the area. Clear away brush and trash, plant as far as you can from attractions such as fruit trees or berry bushes, and so on. If you know of stray cats in the neighborhood of your garden, put out food to attract them. Rats avoid areas that smell of cats.

The most effective prevention is a physical barrier to keep the rats away from the plants. The good news is that because Cannabis isn't a primary food for rats they won't try as hard to get it as they would if they actually liked to eat it. So an effective barrier needs to be at least 18 inches (45 cm) high and have no opening larger than 0.5 inch (12.5 mm. A simple way to meet these requirements is to wrap a tomato cage in chicken wire or hardware cloth and put one of these around each of the plants when you set them out. Another is to buy coarse steel wool (sold in bulk at hardware stores) and wrap it around the stalk of each plant, securing it with twist ties.

Controls

Traps and poison provide protection. Hardware and garden stores carry a variety of effective rat traps. Place traps around the plant cage, and use an attractive bait such as peanut butter. Once a few rats have been trapped, predators may come to enjoy the carrion, making the area unattractive to the rodents.

Rats have begun to develop resistance to warfarin, the classic anti-coagulant "rat poison." Another problem with this poison is that it can kill predators that eat the dead rats. A newer poison is chole-calciferol (Vitamin D3). Another is zinc phosphide. Both are available in various brand name rodent baits. Place any such poison bait in a tamper-proof bait station.

SLUGS AND SNAILS

How common are they?

Snails and slugs occasionally attack outdoor gardens. They are rare indoors.

What does the pest look like?

Slugs range in color from pale gray to tan, and grow to as long as 2 inches (5 cm). Their bodies are soft and fleshy, and glisten with a clear slime that the slugs secrete to retain moisture and help their movement. Two small "horns" atop the slug's head are actually the slug's "eyes" (these merely sense light; slugs have no sense of sight per se).

Snails are slugs with shells. They are built almost identically to slugs, except for a coiled shell of calcium carbonate that protects most of a snail's body. A snail can withdraw completely into its shell when threatened. The shells of common garden snails can reach up to 1.5 inch (3.75 cm) in diameter, and come in various shades of gray, brown, and black, sometimes with markings, depending on the species.

Where the pest is found

Snails and slugs are found on the leaves and edges of leaves and flowers.

What it does to the plant

They eat leaves. Holes in leaves and/or clipped edges of leaves and flowers, accompanied by a silvery, slimy trail, indicate snail or slug damage. A single snail can savage several small plants in one night.

General discussion

These pests thrive in moist, dark environments. They hide in mulch, short and stubby plants, under boards, and in soil, and they avoid sunlight, so they are seldom seen during the day, but come out to feast at night.

There is one particular kind of snail that you should leave alone. So-called "decollate" snails sometimes attack plants, but their main food is other snails and slugs. The fastest way to tell a "good" snail from a plant-eating pest is the shape of the shell: common garden snails usually have round shells that coil in a simple spiral. Most species of decollate snails have cone-shaped shells. If these are the only snails you ever see in your garden, then go ahead and get rid of them, because they eat plants if there is no other food in their habitat. But if you have other snails as well then the decollate snail is your friend.

Reproduction rate and life cycle: Slugs and snails are hermaphroditic, and can fertilize themselves if no mate is available. They lay clutches of 30 to 120 eggs 1-2 inches (2.5 to 5 cm) deep in moist soil. When conditions are suitable (not too dry or too cold) slugs and snails can lay eggs as often as once a month, so their numbers can increase rapidly during damp spring and fall weather.

Prevention and Control

The best way to prevent and kill snails and slugs is with iron phosphate, sometimes called ferric phosphate. It is completely effective and requires little effort. It comes as a powder or granules and is not harmful to plants, pets or humans. Sprinkle on the ground as directed. Many brands are available.

Diatomaceous earth sprinkled around the base of the stems helps keep out slugs and snails, but it can also hinder beneficial insects.

A number of methods can be used to prevent snail or slug damage. Reduce damage dramatically by watering in the morning instead of the evening. The soil has time to dry out and become less attractive to the pests.

Place copper wire, tape or mesh around the garden or at the base of the plants. Copper shocks the pests and deters them (dimes and quarter work as well). When enclosing the garden or plants with copper, make sure not to trap the snails inside.

Slugs love beer! Bury a container of beer in the garden, leaving it just barely above the ground so they can drink it and drown. Salt causes their bodies to shrivel up. Predators such as firefly larva toads, frogs, fireflies, snakes, birds, and black iridescent beetles like snails. Firefly larvae eat slugs and snails viciously. Slugs can be trapped. Construct a cool moist area for them to retreat to during the heat of the day.

SPIDER MITES

Actual Size: 02" • .5 mm

How common is it?

Spider mites are very common. They are the most serious pests in the Cannabis garden.

What does the pest look like?

Spider mites are barely visible with the naked eye since they are only 0.02 inch (0.4mm) long. They are arachnids (relatives of spiders), and like other arachnids they have four pairs of legs and no antennae. Unlike spiders, though, mites have only a single body segment. Their colors can range from red brown and black to yellow and green depending on the species and the time of year. Spider mites are so tiny though that most of these details are visible only with a magnifier.

Where the pest is found

They live on the plants, mostly on the underside the leaves, but can also be found on the buds. They can also be found moving along their silvery webbing, from leaf to leaf and even plant to plant.

What it does to the plant

Spider mites pierce the surface of the leaves, then suck plant juices from them. These punctures appear on the leaves as tiny brown spots surrounded by yellowing leaf.

Identify infestation by tiny spots on the leaves. They can be seen as colored dots on the leaf undersides As the population grows they produce webbing that the mites use as a pedestrian bridge between branches or plants.

Spider mites are also vectors for disease, since they travel from leaf to leaf and further.

How they work

Spider mites are sap-feeders, like many other garden pests. They are more of a threat than most though, due to their high rate of reproduction.

General discussion

Spider mites are by far the most fearsome of all plant pests. They

Spider mites (red circles) and mite eggs (blue circle). *Photo: Sukalo*

suck plant juices, weakening the plants. Spider mites multiply quickly. They are most active in warmer climates than cold ones.

Reproduction rate and life cycle: Newly hatched mites are 3:1 female:male, and each female lays up to 200 eggs. This life cycle can repeat as often as every eight days in warm, dry conditions such as a grow room. This means that a spider mite population can explode with shocking speed, and this rapid reproduction is what makes them so troublesome.

Prevention

Almost all spider mite infestations enter the garden on an infested plant or through the ventilation system, or are introduced by gardeners who carry the hitchhikers into the garden. Use a fine dust filter in the ventilation system, and never enter the grow space wearing clothing that has recently been outdoors, especially in a garden.

Neem oil is often used as a preventative, but always look out for webbing and for the yellow-brown spots mites leave when feeding. Infected mother plants transmit mites on their clones, so it is especially important to watch for mites in a mother room. When you spot mite symptoms take action immediately.

Control

Spider mites thrive in dry climates. High humidity slows spider

Spider mite webbing

mite development and reproduction. This can be used in vegetative and early flowering stages to slow population increase.

- Insecticidal soap smothers many of the mites, lowering the population and the damage, but does not eliminate the population.

- Pyrethrum is effective against some mite populations, but others have developed immunity to it.

- Cinnamon-clove tea can be brewed using powdered cinnamon and clove. Start using about an ounce of each per gallon of water. Boil water. Let stand a couple of minutes. Add the herbs and let brew until the water is cool. Strain.

- Predator mites: There are many varieties. Get those best suited to the environment in your garden. Apply predator mites at the earliest sign of infestation. Most predator species reproduce faster than spider mites, but if the mites get a good head start the predator population can never catch up. Even in optimal conditions control with predator mites is very difficult.

- *Beauveria bassiana* (beneficial fungi)

- Beneficial insects (lady beetles, predatory mites, Minute pirate bugs)

- Capsaicin

- Carbon dioxide

- Cinnamon oil

- Coriander oil

- Fish Oil

Mites congregating

- Garlic
- Herbal Oils
- Horticultural Oil
- Insecticidal soaps
- Limonene
- Neem oil
- *Saccharopolyspora spinosa* (beneficial bacteria)
- Sesame oil

Spider mite damage.

THRIPS

Actual size: 1/15" • 1.5 mm

How common is it?

Thrips are not commonly considered pests of marijuana. However, in some greenhouse conditions they can be serious pests.

What does the pest look like?

Thrips are tiny, no more than 0.06 inch (1.5 mm) long, but can still be seen by the naked eye. Adults have wings but do not fly well; they jump when startled. The head and body range from yellow to dark brown. The larvae are about half the size of adults, lighter in color, and wingless.

Where the pest is found

Thrips attack the leaves and are usually found on the top surface of the leaf.

What it does to the plant

Thrips use a saw-like structure to pierce and scrape the flesh until sap begins to flow. They then suck up the juices, and leave a surface of patchy white or silvery scrapes. The leaf surface looks scarred or scabby. Eventually the leaves look like all the chlorophyll has been drained, and they turn white. Thrips leave behind greenish black specks of poop on and under leaves. The scar tissue shows up in silver patches. Thrip damage can resemble that of spider mites or leaf miners at first, but more severe cases result in the color-stripped leaves.

Damaged leaves can't be healed and their ability to absorb light is compromised. If the thrips are not controlled the plants die. Thrips also carry pathogens that they transfer from plant to plant.

How it works

Thrips pierce the leaves then suck out its contents. Thrips lay eggs on the plants. The larvae drop down to the soil and pupate there.

General discussion

Outdoors, thrips hibernate over the winter in soil and plant debris. Thrips become active when the temperature climbs above 60 °F (16 °C). The warm, stable temperatures of indoor gardens allow them to be active year-round. Thrips are a more serious problem indoors

Thrips in different stages of development. *Photos: (top) Bob91, (bottom) 01flat*

because of this, and also because a natural soil-dwelling fungus that infects thrips pupae is not present indoors.

Reproduction rate and life cycle: Females lay eggs (anywhere from 40 to 300 depending on species) in plant crevices or actually insert them into the leaves and stems. The larvae feed until they enter the pupal stage, when they fall to the ground (and when the soil fungi provide some biocontrol outdoors). Depending on the species and temperature (optimum is 77 to 82°F (26 to 28°C)), the larval thrips hatch, pupate, and mature to egg-laying adults in 7 to 30 days.

Prevention

Thrips are drawn to the colors blue and yellow, so it's best to avoid having yellow walls or items around your Cannabis gardens. Yellow and blue sticky cards can be used as indicator traps to detect an infestation of thrips. Use garlic in outdoor gardens to deter/repel thrips.

Control

- Barrier: Thrips pupae live in the soil after they drop from the plant. By placing a collar around the top of the container, the pupae can't get to the soil and they die. As with fungus gnat larvae, a layer of diatomaceous earth on top of the soil also helps to destroy the thrips pupae.

- *Beauveria bassiana* (beneficial fungi)

- Beneficial Nematodes: if there are beneficial nematodes present they attack the pupae in the soil.

- Capsaicin

- Carbon dioxide

- Cinnamon oil

- Clove Oil

- Coriander oil

- Horticultural oil

- Insecticidal Soaps

- Minute Pirate Bugs (Orius): these insects are tiny but they attack adult thrips. They work well with nematodes.

- Neem oil

- Predatory mites

- Pyrethrum

- *Saccharopolyspora spinosa* (beneficial bacteria)

Thrips infestation. *Photo: Sukalo*

WHITEFLIES

1/16" • 1.5 mm

How common is it?

Whiteflies are a common pest indoors and outdoors.

What does the pest look like?

Whiteflies resemble tiny moths but are neither moths nor true flies. They are relatives of aphids and scales. They are 0.04 inch (1 mm) long and their soft bodies are covered in a powdery wax which gives them protection and their white color.

Where the pest is found

Whiteflies infest the undersides of leaves. If the plant is disturbed they take wing and a mass of tiny white flies can be seen fluttering around the plant.

What does it do to the plant

They suck sap from the plants, and are vectors for viruses. The plants release sticky honeydew and this can contribute to mold problems on the plants. Leaves appear spotty, droop, and lose vigor.

How it works

Whiteflies are sap-feeders, like their relatives, aphids and scales.

General discussion

Whiteflies are a pest in big numbers, but are not difficult to get rid of. If you think the plants might have whiteflies but are unsure, shake the plants a bit. You'll see them flying off, then settling right back onto the leaves.

Reproduction rate and life cycle: Females each lay about 100 tiny eggs on the undersides of leaves. Eggs hatch in about seven to ten days, and the larvae drain sap from leaves. Larvae mature in 2 to 4 weeks and the adults live for 4 to 6 weeks after that. The reproductive rate is temperature dependent: most whitefly species do best in a temperature range of 80 to 90°F (27 to 33°C).

Prevention

Keep the temperature of the garden below 80°F (27°C) to slow whitefly reproduction. Clear out plant debris quickly. Install a fine dust filter in the air intake for the grow space to prevent whiteflies from entering through the vents.

Control

- Yellow Sticky Traps- Whiteflies are attracted to yellow sticky cards. These trap a small proportion of the population, but are good indicators of infestations.

- Shake plants to dislodge whiteflies and then suck them out of the air with the hose attachment of a vacuum cleaner. Heavily infested plants should be removed from the garden or grow room before treatment.

- *Encarsia formosae* are tiny wasps that lay their eggs inside immature whiteflies. They are not social, they don't make hives and are so small that once they are released you may never see them again. Indoors and in greenhouses one introduction may be all that is needed because their numbers increase much faster proportionally than their prey.

- *Beauveria bassiana* (beneficial fungi)

- Beneficial insects (lacewing larvae, minute pirate bugs)

- Capsaicin

- Carbon dioxide

- Cinnamon oil

Whiteflies and eggs. *Photo: Digital Hippy*

Whiteflies. *Photo: Digital Hippy*

- Cloves
- Coriander oil
- Garlic
- Herbal Oils
- Horticultural Oil
- Insecticidal soap
- Limonene
- Neem oil
- Parasitoid Wasps
- Pyrethrum
- Sesame oil

SECTION 3 DISEASES

Disease can strike marijuana plants at any stage. Most diseases that affect marijuana fall into two broad categories: fungal and bacterial. The spores and bacteria that cause plant diseases are actually ubiquitous. A garden's susceptibility to disease is often traceable to environmental imbalances in temperature, moisture, light conditions, airflow, and pH among others.

Fungus grows when it finds the right levels of moisture, temperature (the range varies by species), acidic conditions, and a reliable source of food.

Bacteria are much more likely to invade when the environment has been compromised, in conditions such as oxygen deprivation, which make their attack more successful.

Once disease hits, it is important to act quickly and restore balance to the environment. However, prevention by providing a balanced environment for the plants is the best solution.

AIR FILTRATION AND SANITATION

Fungal spores often enter a growspace on air currents. A fine dust filter in the air intake system captures these spores and reduces the chance of fungal infections. Another option is a UVC lamp in the intake duct. The light from these lamps kills microbes and destroys spores. The two options can be combined.

ALGAE

Algae are plant like, usually microscopic organisms. Some are unicellular and others form multi celled organisms. They conduct photosynthesis like larger plants, but lack stems, roots and leaves.

How common is it?

Algae occasionally grow in hydroponic and aeroponic systems.

Origin

Algae thrive in environments that provide warm temperature, light and nutrients. The water temperature should be 72° F (22° C), which is best for maximum plant growth. Unfortunately it is also a good temperature for algae.

When light shines on nutrient-rich water, algae are almost guaranteed to grow.

Where the disease is found

Algae can grow anywhere in your system. It is commonly found inside tubes, nutrient reservoirs, buckets, on exposed rock wool cube surfaces, and DWC buckets (mainly if the containers are not opaque and allow light in.

All containers should be opaque.

Appearance and effect of the disease

Some algae attach to surfaces such as tubes and reservoir surfaces as well as roots. They form a green film that looks and feels either velvety or slimy. When it covers the roots it starves them of oxygen. It also competes for nutrients and can clog your system lines, motors, and sprayers in aeroponics systems.

Other algae are free-swimming and don't attach themselves to surfaces. These algae can also clog up tubing.

Both kinds of algae photosynthesize during the day, using CO_2 dissolved in the water and releasing oxygen (O_2). However, during the dark period algae use oxygen dissolved in the water and release CO_2. This depletes the water of oxygen, which the roots require to maintain health.

Prevention

The best way to prevent algae is to deprive it of light. This is a safe, non-chemical method of prevention. Use black tubing, rather than clear or translucent to prevent light from coming into the lines. Use a black or opaque reservoir to hold your water and nutrients. Make sure the cover is light-tight. Potting containers should be opaque.

Everything should be light-proof. Rock wool cubes should also be covered. You can use landscape sun-block fabric, white-black plastic (white side up) or plastic rock wool cube covers made for the purpose.

Control

The best method of algae control is to prevent the problem by excluding light. This should be the main emphasis in systems with algae problems. If you already have algae growing, clean the system and replace or cover light transmitting tubing and reservoirs with opaque materials.

Algae growth. *Photo: Asher1er*

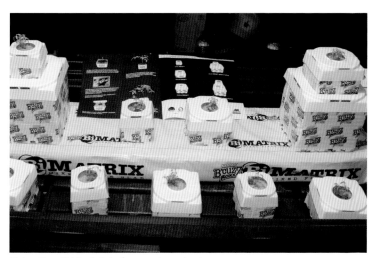

Cube Caps® block light from rockwool cubes.

These are some products you can use to control or prevent algae from attacking the system:

- H_2O_2—A ½ to 1% hydrogen peroxide solution will stop algae and other organisms but must be used regularly. It should not be used with mycorrhizae because H_2O_2 kills both good and bad micro-organisms.

- Colloidal silver—A solution of a few parts per million (ppm) colloidal silver prevents algae growth and like H_2O_2 it kills all micro-organisms.

- UVC light—This is considered a germicidal light and is often used to keep hot tubs, fish tanks and other water free from micro-organisms.

- Grapefruit seed extract—Grapefruit seed extract kills algae without harming plants. This method is used by water supply systems for keeping drinking water, fish ponds and lakes algae free.

- Barley straw rafts measuring inches across are used for algae control in ponds, lakes and other waterways. They can also be placed in hydroponic reservoirs.

GRAY MOLD AND BROWN MOLD (BOTRYTIS)

Gray mold, *Botrytis cinerea*, is found almost everywhere and can cause disease on most plants, including marijuana. It can cause damping off and stem canker but is most serious when it causes bud rot.

How common is it?

Gray mold is one of the most common fungal diseases that attack marijuana.

Origin

The fungus can germinate only on wet plant tissue when the temperature is between 55-70° F (13-21° C). This often happens in dry weather as dew accumulates on the leaves. Once it starts growing it can tolerate a wide range of humidity and temperatures but high humidity and cool temperatures help it thrive. Lowering the humidity often stops it from continuing to grow.

Gray mold, like most other fungi, enters and easily infects any part of a plant that is either wounded, damaged from pests and pruning, or beginning to die. Thus it is very important to sanitize pruning equipment between cuts.

Cuts and lesions are a normal part of plant life, so all plants are

Grey mold. *Photo: Ed Rosenthal*

subject to attack when conditions are favorable to the mold. Unhealthy or shaded areas of plants or crevices in buds are ideal conditions for the mold. Spores travel mostly via wind and rain and even in tap water, but they can be brought into grow rooms on clothing and pets.

Where the disease is found

Shaded areas of the plant that do not get a lot of light are usually first infected. Then the disease spreads quickly through growth and spores.

Gray mold does the greatest amount of damage during flowering. It attacks the flowering tops, leaves, and stalks. Seedlings and seeds can also be infected and killed.

Appearance and effect of the disease

The mold starts out whitish like powdery mildew, but then darkens to a smoky gray or brown color. It has a fuzzy appearance, and light to dark brown rot forms in the damaged tissue.

Leaves and buds yellow from being suffocated by the mold. In higher humidity, the gray mold leaves a brown slimy substance on the leaves and turns the bud to rot, especially when the tissue is dense late in flowering.

Stems with unhealed breaks can be infected with B. cinerea causing stem cankers, which then affect the rest of the plant by depriving it of nutrients and water.

Grey mold

Moldy bud.

Prevention

Indoors, avoid conditions favorable to the mold by controlling humidity and temperature. Keep humidity under 50%. Water when your grow lights are on or during the day. Remove and discard dead or dying plant tissue. Make sure there is no moisture on leaves and buds when the lights go out. Gray mold indoors is usually caused by high humidity.

Outdoors, you can't control the weather but you can prevent bud rot. *Bacillus subtilis* is a bacterium that attacks *B. cinerea*. It can be sprayed on the plant as a preventative.

Potassium bicarbonate ($KHCO_3$) and pH Up change the pH of the environment to alkaline from acidic. Alkaline environments inhibit the germination of molds and fungi including gray mold.

Sulfur is often used to control fungi, and is used as a spray or vapor.

Neem oil and sesame oil form a barrier and inhibit mold germination.

Control

If you see the mold or stem wounds, apply a fungicide. The mold is particularly difficult to remove from plants in late flowering.

Removing the mold from living bud to prevent its spread may do more harm than good unless done carefully. The very act of fiddling with them may help transfer the mold to new sites. Sterilize tools by dipping them in alcohol or hydrogen peroxide after curing a bud.

Bud mold.

- *Bacillus pumilus* (beneficial bacteria)
- Clove oil
- Compost and compost tea
- Copper
- Coriander oil
- Neem oil
- Potassium bicarbonate
- *Pseudomonas* (beneficial bacteria)
- Quaternary amines
- Sesame and fish oil
- Sodium bicarbonate
- Sulfur: spray, vaporizer, or burner
- *Trichoderma* (beneficial fungi)

LEAF SEPTORIA

Leaf Septoria is also known as yellow leaf spot. It is not common indoors but occasionally attacks marijuana grown outdoors. The fungus interferes with leaf processes, including photosynthesis, inhibiting a plant's ability to thrive. Though it is not deadly, it can greatly reduce yield.

Origin

Two closely related fungi, *Septoria cannabis* and *S. neocannabina*, cause yellow leaf spot. Yellow leaf spot is a wet and cloudy warm weather infection. Warm water and rain trigger the release of spores from the storage structures so it usually appears mid to late season. Infections occur when the temperature is in the 60's, but the fungi grow faster and are more destructive as the temperature rises, with its ideal temperature just below 80° F (25° C).

Where the disease is found

The spots first appear on the lower leaves of the plant. The fungus may also attack the stem.

Appearance and effect of the disease

The spots can be yellow, white, or gray-brown. They may remain small and round, but usually grow larger in an irregular pattern.

Leaf septoria. *Photo: Og Royal Grower*

Leaf septoria. *Photos: (top) Og Royal Grower, (bottom) Ldm*

Spots sometimes have reddish-brown perimeters. The infected tissue eventually dies and dries out and falls off, resulting in holes in the leaves. Severe infections result in defoliation, with no leaves left on the bottom of the plant.

Prevention

The Septoria fungi are specific but ubiquitous. Only two species attack Cannabis. As a result, plants are more likely to be infected if there is marijuana, or perhaps hops, growing outdoors near the garden. The spores overwinter on fallen infected marijuana leaves and debris and spread in three ways: wind, water and walking, either by humans and animals. Indoors, plants are not likely to come in contact with the spores unless they are trekked in or there are infected outdoor plants nearby.

Outdoors, infections are most likely to occur in gardens and spaces where marijuana has been grown before. To lessen the likelihood of infection remove all residue from the previous garden and then spray the area with a fungicide. Clean and decontaminate all tools after working with infected plants. If possible plant the garden in a different space each year.

- *Bacillus pumilis* (beneficial bacteria)
- Cinnamon and clove oils
- Compost and compost tea
- Copper
- Coriander oil
- Neem oil
- pH Up
- Potassium bicarbonate
- Sesame and fish oils
- Sodium bicarbonate
- *Trichoderma* (beneficial fungi)

Control

- Prune away infected leaves and branches to remove infection vectors.
- Neem oil
- Copper fungicides, including Bordeaux mixture, can slow the disease.
- Sulfur

POWDERY MILDEW

Powdery mildew is a fungal disease that affects a wide range of plants, composed of a wide variety of species. Each species of powdery mildew has a very limited host range, but are all characterized by an easily recognizable white or gray powdery growth. The races that attack hops also attack marijuana.

How common is it?

Mildew spores can be found everywhere. Powdery mildew is a common problem for both indoor and outdoor growers whenever the temperature and humidity fall into its favored range.

Origin

Mildew spores are ubiquitous and endemic. In areas where marijuana or hops is being grown wind and air ventilation are the main vectors. Another major factor is contaminated cuttings. However, clothing, pets, and outdoor animals can also deliver spores to the garden.

Spores can remain dormant until environmental factors, which include a suitable host, adequate humidity, moderate temperatures, low light intensity and acidity trigger them.

Where the disease is found

Powdery mildew is most likely to attack young leaves, up to two or three weeks old. The infection spreads over the plant and spreads to other plants in the garden. It affects buds, stems, stalks, and

Powdery Mildew. *Photo: Ed Rosenthal*

Powdery Mildew. *Photo: Beach Stoned*

leaves.

Appearance and effect of the disease

The first signs of an infection are raised humps on the upper leaf surfaces. Plant leaves look like they've been dusted with flour or confectionary sugar. At first it might appear on just a small portion of the leaf in an irregular circle pattern. It quickly spreads and soon the entire leaf is covered as if it had been powdered.

Infected plants prematurely yellow, brown, and eventually die. If untreated, black specks can arise in the white powdery mildew. Buds have a stale, moist smell and are coated with the white powdery-

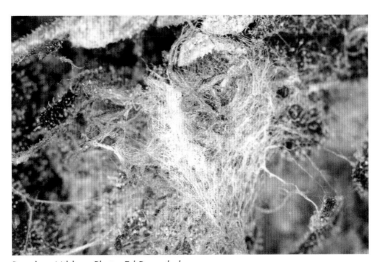

Powdery Mildew. *Photo: Ed Rosenthal*

looking mildew substance that can't be removed. Powdery mildew hinders photosynthesis, causing your harvest to cripple to little or no yield.

Infected buds and leaves are not acceptable for smoking.

Prevention

Powdery mildew in vegetative growth is easier to treat than in the later stages of flowering. Quarantine all new plants in a separate area where they can't infect other plants. If your plants get infected during flowering, especially far into the flowering stage, the buds will eventually become infected.

Filter incoming air to prevent spores from entering the room in the airstream. A germicidal UVC light like the ones used in food handling kills powdery mildew spores that are airborne. Ionizers and ozone generators precipitate and inactivate spores, lessening the chances of infection.

As with other fungi, restrict humidity and spore production not by watering or foliar spraying at night or with lights off. Water plants when lights first come on or with at least five hours of remaining light time. Keep humidity in check; anything over 50% may trigger problems. Keep plants spaced apart to allow for maximum airflow in between plants helps to minimize plant-to-plant infection.

To prevent outbreaks you can use the following products on a regular basis:

Powdery Mildew. *Photo: Ed Rosenthal*

Powdery Mildew. *Photo: Big Green Budder*

- *Ampelomyces quisqualis* (beneficial fungi)
- *Bacillus pumilis* (beneficial bacteria)
- *Bacillus subtilis* (beneficial bacteria)
- Compost and compost tea
- Milk
- Neem oil
- Potassium bicarbonate
- Sesame and fish oils
- Sodium bicarbonate

Control

Removing infected leaves from the grow room is critical. Carefully remove them without knocking spores into the air. Place a bag over infected leaves and tic it shut; then remove the leaves. Use a fungicide on wounded stems from which you've removed the leaves.

The following product list will work for indoor and outdoor plants.

- Vinegar
- *Bacillus pumilis* (beneficial bacteria)
- *Bacillus subtilis* (beneficial bacteria)
- Cinnamon Oil and Tea

- Clove Oil
- Copper
- Coriander Oil
- Garlic
- Horticultural oils containing jojoba or cottonseed oil
- Hydrogen peroxide
- Limonene
- Milk
- Neem oil
- pH Up
- Potassium bicarbonate
- Sesame oil
- Sodium bicarbonate
- Sulfur

ROOT DISEASES

Every plant must have a healthy root system. Pathogens can attack and damage the roots of one plant, then rapidly infect other plants in the garden. Fusarium, Verticillium and Pythium are common and destructive root aggressors known to all growers, whether soil gardeners or hydroponicists.

FUSARIUM

Fusarium inhabits the soil. Fusarium fungi vary across many species and subspecies, and a given strain of the fungus targets only a few plant species. Several strains target Cannabis. Fusarium is so devastating that the US government has developed special strains to target Cannabis and coca as part of the "War on Drugs." The coca strain has been released on coca plants in Colombia.

Different Fusarium species produce somewhat different diseases in Cannabis. These diseases, primarily Fusarium wilt and Fusarium root rot, present different symptoms but respond to similar prevention and control methods.

How common is it?

It is not commonly found in marijuana gardens. However residual spores are more common in soil where hemp was once grown or where it still grows as a weed. Growers using hydroponic systems or sterile or pasteurized planting mix seldom see it. Fusarium infections are most common in warm weather, but overall the frequency varies. Because it is soil-based and species-specific it may

Fusarium wilt. *Photos: Hort*

Fusarium wilt. *Photo: Hort*

be extremely common in one area but rare in another where the soil is not infected.

Origin

Fusarium spores can remain dormant in soil for years, and infected soil is nearly impossible to disinfect. The fungus can also spread from seed taken from infected plants.

Where the disease is found

Damage from Fusarium wilt is most evident on the leaves and stems. Fusarium root rot affects the roots first, then the disease works its way up the stem.

Appearance and effect of the disease

Fusarium wilt initially appears as small, dark irregular spots on lower leaves, which quickly become chlorotic (yellow-brown). Leaf tips curl upward, and wilted leaves dry and hang on plants without falling off. Stems turn yellow, then brown, and finally collapse. In Fusarium wilt the roots show no outward symptoms if the diseased plant is pulled up.

Fusarium root rot begins below the soil line, turning the roots rotten and necrotic and giving them a characteristic red color. The first visible symptom usually appears as the rot works its way up the stem, producing a red-brown discoloration at the soil line. This discoloration may progress to swelling and the stem may split open. The plant soon begins to wilt, then collapses as the decay spreads up the stalk.

In both wilt and root rot the fungus spreads through plant cells and clogs the xylem vessels, inhibiting water and nutrient transport. This vascular clogging inside the plants causes the external symptoms of wilt and collapse. Infected plants usually die. Fusarium survives in the plant debris, so infected plant debris should not be buried, composted, or placed on uninfected soil.

Prevention

If an outdoor Cannabis crop falls prey to Fusarium, that patch of ground can no longer be used to grow Cannabis at all, although other plants will do fine there. Likewise seeds produced by infected plants should not be used. The pathogen stays dormant on the seed and attacks the plant when the seedling emerges, causing damping off and likely killing it.

Avoid planting marijuana in the same ground for many years in a row. Even though none of the plants show symptoms, multiple successive plantings can cause the fungus to build up in the soil until it reaches destructive levels.

Certain soil types have been found to be less conducive to the growth of Fusarium than others. Clay soils have fungistatic prop-

Root rot. *Photo: Chemical Burn*

erties due to their high pH. Loamy soils with healthy and diverse plant growth often harbor native microbes that suppress Fusarium. These soils do not stop the fungus, but they slow it down, and may be helpful in combination with other preventive measures.

Properly aged compost, and tea made from compost, help protect plants from all sorts of fungal infections.

Container gardening is one of the best ways to avoid Fusarium, because it gives the gardener complete control over the soil. If an area that would otherwise be ideal (weather, sun, etc.) is known to be infected with Fusarium then containers allow you to take advantage of the site's strong points while avoiding the disease issues. In order to prevent Fusarium infections, use sterilized or pasteurized soil mixes and new pots, and do not over-fertilize. Make sure the soil drains.

Mycorrhizae (beneficial fungi) help improve plants' disease resistance.

Streptomyces griseoviridis, Bacillus pumilus, and *Bacillus subtilis* (all beneficial bacteria) or *Gliocladium* (beneficial fungus) can be applied as pretreatments for seeds, as a soil drench, or as a foliar spray.

Make sure the soil pH doesn't get too low. Neutralize acidic soil with dolomite lime or greensand. Fertilizers enhanced with potassium and calcium can help fight off and prevent Fusarium, while excess nitrogen and phosphorous may make the disease worse.

Control

The only truly effective control is the removal and destruction of infected plants. After removing any affected plants use hydrogen peroxide (H_2O_2) to clean all the tools that touched those plants before using them again.

VERTICILLIUM WILT

How common is it?

Verticillium wilt is caused by soil-borne fungi that are common in many soils, and it attacks hundreds of herbaceous and woody plant species, including Cannabis.

Origin

Verticillium wilt thrives in moist soil that is rich in clay or otherwise poorly drained.

Where the disease is found

Verticillium wilt starts by attacking stressed roots then proceeds to affect the leaves as well.

Appearance and effect of the disease

The lower leaves turn yellow along the margins and between the veins before turning a gray-brown and wilting. The stem turns brown near the soil line; symptoms can resemble Fusarium wilt. Once the roots have been affected, it spreads through the xylem, which exhibits a brownish discoloration. The vascular system becomes plugged up, which reduces the flow of water through the roots and causes the wilting.

Prevention

Sterile planting mix or hydroponic growing systems prevents Verticillium infection. However any amount of soil in the growing containers may carry the fungus. Many soil bacteria and fungi help to suppress Verticillium, so if sterile soil isn't an option then amending your soil with alfalfa meal or aged compost may offer

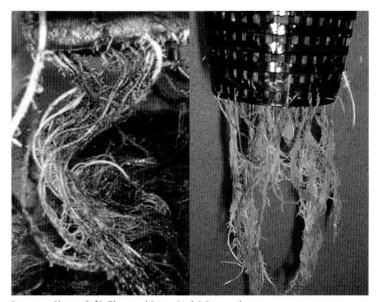

Root rot. *Photo: (left) Chemical Burn, (right) Diggerdigzit*

some protection. Keep the planting beds well drained, as excess moisture in the root zone greatly increases the risk of Verticillium.

Properly aged compost, and tea made from compost, help protect plants from all sorts of fungal infections.

Control

There is no chemical control available. The best thing to do is pasteurize the soil. A fertilizer that is low in nitrogen and high in potassium may help. Some possible biocontrols include:

- *Bacillus subtilis* (FZB24 strain)
- *Trichoderma* fungus

PYTHIUM

Pythium is a destructive parasitic root fungus. Under favorable conditions Pythium multiplies very rapidly and releases microscopic spores that infect the roots and deprive the plant of food. It attacks mainly seeds and seedlings, which have little resistance to disease. Larger plants can be treated and saved, if they are identified early, although your crop will be stunted.

How common is it?

Pythium is a common problem in field, container, and hydroponic cultivation.

Origin

Pythium exists everywhere in the plant's environment. It is present in your growing area, no matter how clean it is. Sanitation still helps: Pythium is often described as a "secondary infection," because it attacks plants that have already been weakened by stress: disease, damage, pests, nutrient deficiencies or poor growing conditions. Providing a healthy growing environment helps to prevent infection.

The best conditions for Pythium development include high moisture levels in the soil, high humidity, and a temperature between 70 and 85° F (20 to 30° C). Lack of oxygen in hydroponic nutrient solutions also helps Pythium take hold.

Where the disease is found

Pythium generally affects the entire plant, but mainly the roots and foliage. Young plants and seedlings in both soil fields and hydroponic gardens are the most susceptible.

Appearance and effect of the disease

Look for an overall yellowing of the foliage, sometimes accompanied by browning leaf edges. The plant appears wilted or stunted. The roots become discolored, soft, and watery. As the infection advances, the outer part of the roots comes off exposing a stringy inner core. In soil gardens and containers the roots will not be visible, but Pythium often advances from the roots to the "crown" of the plant, just above the soil line, causing the same browning and softening that it produces in the roots.

Pythium moves through soil or water to the plant roots where it germinates before entering the roots. Once in the roots it spreads through the tissue and produces resting spores, which further germinate and can infect the roots indirectly.

Prevention

The best prevention is keeping the plants healthy and free of other pests that might give Pythium an opening. Use well-drained, pasteurized soil or soilless mixes in containers and avoid over-fertilization and over-watering. Address pests, other diseases, and nutrient deficiencies promptly, as these stresses make plants more susceptible to Pythium.

Properly aged compost, and tea made from compost, help protect plants from all sorts of fungal infections.

Keep fungus gnats in check, as they can carry Pythium spores into containers with pasteurized soil. Note that one of the preventive measures for fungus gnats is to let the soil dry to a depth of about 1 inch (2-3 cm) between waterings, which reduces Pythium growth.

Prevention is especially important in hydroponic systems. Once Pythium infects these systems it may spread through the water too quickly to stop. Keep your system as clean as possible to avoid infection.

An option for very thorough cleaning is to treat the water with hydrogen peroxide (H_2O_2) at each nutrient solution change. UVC water disinfection systems kill water-borne spores. However, these methods kill beneficial organisms in the nutrient solution as well as pathogens like Pythium. The value of this trade-off varies from one system to the next, but it is worthwhile for some growers.

Biocontrols such as those listed below are effective if applied before the plant shows any symptoms. Note that disinfection measures such as peroxide and UVC in hydroponic systems will also kill off these biocontrol agents.

- *Bacillus subtilis* (beneficial bacteria)
- *Gliocladium* (beneficial fungus)
- *Pseudomonas* (beneficial bacteria)
- *Streptomyces griseoviridis* (beneficial bacteria)

Controls

Pythium presents very similar symptoms to Phytophthora root rot in plants other than Cannabis. However while Phytophthora is a common problem in many other plants, no species is known to infect Cannabis. Therefore marijuana gardeners should verify that any control they use is listed for use against Pythium. Controls that are specific for Phytophthora are not effective.

- Copper
- Clove oil
- Coriander oil
- Quaternary amines
- Sesame oil
- *Trichoderma* (beneficial fungi)

STEM ROTS—DAMPING OFF

Damping off is a condition rather than a specific disease: the rotting of seedlings either underground, at the soil line, or at the crown. It is caused by several seed- and soil-born fungi, especially Rhizoctonia and Pythium. Damping off mainly affects soil growers and generally kills any seedling it affects.

How common is it?

Damping off is a common problem. It is often blamed on bad seeds, as it may destroy the seedlings even before they emerge from the grow medium.

Origin

Damping off occurs in warm, nitrogen-rich soil that stays wet for long periods. Even hydroponics systems can get damping off when the growing media become too saturated.

Where the disease is found

The infection begins below the soil line and affects seedlings with up to eight sets of true leaves or three leaf nodes. Leaves, roots, and stems can be affected.

Appearance and effect of the disease

Damping off begins as a yellowish-brown discoloration on the lower portion of the stalk. Stems have brown lesions and eventually a dark reddish-brown sunken canker. Cankers form mostly on the stems, between nodes. The third, fourth, and fifth nodes are affected most frequently. As the disease progresses, the lower part of the stem becomes soft and brown. Eventually the underdeveloped plant simply falls over.

The wilting may resemble root rot when the plant first starts to wilt and the leaves turn yellow, but stem canker has not yet appeared. The key difference from root rot is that in damping off the roots are not affected.

In the later stages of damping off in vegetative seedlings, the leaves droop and turn yellow, as if the plant was over watered. As lesions extend up the plant, it begins to wilt due to vascular damage (see the entry on Pythium for more information on this).

Damping-off can easily be mistaken for excessive fertilization (nutrient burn), high levels of salts in the soil, nutrient solution buildup in hydroponic systems, excessive heat or cold, or excessive or insufficient soil moisture. A key diagnostic sign is the brown discoloration near the soil line.

Prevention

The best preventives for damping off all focus on keeping your soil from getting too wet. Although it is always possible to over-water, these measures greatly reduce damping off.

Use a planting mix that includes a generous amount of perlite or vermiculite. This gives the excess water a chance to drain.

Make sure the soil surface is dry before watering. Use a moisture meter or a "finger test" to test soil moisture. Testing the soil near the edge of the pot is less likely to disturb root development.

Place the seeds no deeper than ¼ inch. Soil is wetter further down.

Apply a fungicide to the seeds before planting to minimize post-emergence damping off. Don't transplant seedlings outside until they have several sets of leaves, as younger plants don't yet have a robust root system or resistance to disease.

Properly aged compost, and tea made from compost, help protect plants from all sorts of fungal infections.

Nitrogen-rich soils hinder root growth and aggravate damping off. Soil-less planting mixtures drain well and deter fungus growth. Using sterile soil helps greatly.

Keep the grow room and tools clean, and keep the plants free of pests. This helps to prevent damping off just as it helps against other fungal diseases.

- *Bacillus subtilis* (beneficial bacteria)
- *Gliocladium* (beneficial fungus)
- *Pseudomonas* (beneficial bacteria)
- *Streptomyces griseoviridis* (beneficial bacteria)

Control

There is very little chance of saving seedlings that are struck by damping off soon after they germinate. Vegetative-stage plants with a few sets of leaves have a better chance of fighting it off with the help of fungicide.

Catching the problem early makes your growing life easier. As with other fungal diseases, remove infected areas of the plant entirely and treat the resulting wounds with hydrogen peroxide (H_2O_2). If the stem canker becomes severe then foliar feeding is a must to maintain the plants' vigor, strength, and stamina for the fight.

- Copper
- Clove oil
- Coriander oil
- Quaternary amines
- Sesame oil
- *Trichoderma* (beneficial fungi)

Healthy garden. *Photo: Ed Rosenthal*

SECTION 4 ENVIRONMENTAL STRESSES

Temperature, humidity, air quality and the amount and type of light all affect your garden's health and yield. Whether growing indoors or outdoors the grower must do as much as possible to optimize the environment the plants grow in. The problems discussed in this section are mainly caused by grower error. You get details on how to fix each mistake and how to avoid its recurrence.

Indicas and Sativas

Most commonly grown strains of cannabis are sativa, indica, or a hybrid of the two. Sativas have long skinny leaves; indicas have short, fat, stubby leaves. You can tell by looking at the plant whether the plant has more sativa or indica. Sativa-dominant have long thin fingers shaped leaves coming from the petiole. Indica-dominant have broader, slightly shorter leaves. Indicas are darker green in color. Both adapt differently to certain environmental factors. Indoor-adapted indicas can bleach from intense light. Sativas can handle more intense light. Sativas take much longer to finish, while indicas ripen faster.

AIRY, LOOSE BUDS

Problem: The buds are airy and loose.

Solution: Airy, loose buds are caused by either lack of light, high temperature during their growth period or by lack of nutrients.

Indoors, high temperature in the garden space or just near the light causes the buds to grow airy and lanky. Move the buds farther from the light so the temperature they experience is no higher than 80°F (27°C). Keep the temperature in the growing space and canopy no higher than 80°.

Outdoors, high temperature during flowering results in loose buds. This is not usually a problem when plants flower in autumn, when the temperature cools. However, when they flower early (because

Airy buds. *Photo: Ananympous*

Airy buds. *Photo: Ananympous*

they are early flowering varieties or because of forcing using light deprivation) this may be a problem. One solution is to lower the temperature in the outdoor garden using a micro-sprayer system often used to cool outdoor living spaces. A powerful pump or high water pressure creates an ultra-fine spray, consisting of droplets that are five microns or less. These evaporate, lowering air temperature in the immediately surrounding area without leaving any moisture on the plants. Micro-spray cleaners are commonly used in greenhouses and patios. They use small amounts of water and are easy to install and operate.

Plants that are not receiving enough light during flowering grow airy buds that don't dense up and mature incompletely. The lighter-weight buds are not as potent because they develop fewer trichomes, which are not as large as they would be under full light. Plants that don't receive enough Potassium during flowering cannot grow abundant flowers. Increase Potassium during mid- and late-flowering.

Airy buds. *Photo: Ananympous*

BROKEN STEMS AND BRANCHES

Problem: Sometimes stems that are heavy with buds tear away from the plant at the joint where the stem and branch are attached, especially during rain or windstorms. Another problem is that some varieties have a weak spot at the joint and some of the lower branches tear away as a matter of course.

Solution: Broken stems and branches that are still attached to the plant can often be repaired using a splint to keep the parts together and for support. Realign the two pieces and tape each part to the support. A stick, piece of wood or other strong material can be used as a splint. Grafting wax can be used at the break to prevent infection and promote growth.

Plants can be protected from breaking by wrapping a plastic net loosely around them so that neither wind nor rain can pull or tear the branches. Supporting the stem using a sturdy stake keeps the plant upright and relieves the stem of additional pressure.

CLONES

Problem: The cuttings won't root.

Solution: Rooting machines make it easy to root cuttings. However, rooting cuttings is not difficult. Trim healthy cuttings from desirable plants. They should be between 6 and 8 inches (15 to 20 cm) long. Trim off most of the leaves making sure to leave the top leaves on. Dip the cutting in rooting gel or powder and then stick it in sterile soil or planting mix, rock wool or Oasis® cubes. Keep the temperature at about 72-75ºF (22-24ºC). The roots should appear in 8-12 days. If you are only rooting a few clones you might try rooting them in water.

To keep the medium sterile and increase oxygen in the water, which promotes rooting, make a solution of one part drug store hydrogen peroxide (3%) with 5 parts water. Initially, give the cuttings 10 Watts of cool white fluorescent per square foot. The clones should be kept in a space with 65% humidity or higher. A dome or cover is an easy way to maintain high humidity. Remove covers after 5-6 days, and keep the clones in an area with high humidity.

After about five days add flowering formula fertilizer at one quarter strength. Increase the light intensity to 20 Watts per square foot. Over the next ten days increase the strength of the nutrients by adding grow formula. The roots should be visible within two weeks of starting.

Varieties differ in how easily and how long they take to root.

Algae can also gunk up clones growing in water, causing them not to grow. To prevent this, use dark-colored opaque container to hold the water.

Problem: Can I take cuttings from a flowering plant? What about a ripe plant?

Solution: Flowering plants, even ripe ones, can be cloned. If possible, take the cutting from a shaded area so that the bud isn't as developed as the outside buds. Woody stems should be avoided when picking clones; the harder the stem the harder it is for the clone to root. Trim as much of the flower off as you can while leaving green leaves on the cutting. Set the cutting in the medium. Keep the light on continuously. It will start to root and the new upper growth with be vegetative rather than flowers.

ELONGATED SEEDLINGS

See *Stretching*.

FLUORESCENT BURN

Problem: A few of the plant's leaves were touching the fluorescent light and they are burned.

Solution: When growing using fluorescents keep the plants a couple of inches (about 5 cm) away from the tubes. Occasionally the

Examples of fluorescent burn. *Photos: (top) Mosfed, (bottom) Toddicus*

leaves will touch and if not moved, the leaves will brown where they were touching the light and exposed to the heat. Occasional light damage won't harm the plant. If the leaf is no longer viable remove it from the plant. If it happens regularly place a wire barrier around the tube so the leaves cannot touch the lamp.

FORCING FLOWERING

Problem: Forcing flowering is not working. The plants won't flower even though the light cycle was turned to 12 hours darkness/12 hours of light several weeks ago.

Solution: Either the light has remained on, there are light leaks into the room or the light was turned on during the dark period. If you have to go into the garden during the dark period you can use a green light in the garden without interrupting the light cycle.

GROW ROOM CONDITIONS

HUMID GROW SPACE

Problem: The grow space is very humid.

Solution: The garden space is humid because the plants emit moisture and it is accumulating in the garden space. The moisture must be removed. The easiest way is to ventilate it out and replace it with drier air. If the garden is a closed system you can use a dehumidifier. This appliance features cold tubing that condenses the moisture from the air. The problem with them is that they release heat and can make the space too hot. Air vent tubing can be affixed to the exhaust so the hot air is directed out of the space.

If the room is already running hot, an air-conditioner can be used to remove the moisture as it cools the garden.

HOT GROW ROOM

Problem: The grow room is too hot.

Solution: There are a few ways to cool down a hot grow space.

- It can be ventilated to remove the heat.

- An air-conditioner can be used to remove the heat from the air.

- Before flowering an air cooler that evaporates water to cool the room can be used. It does not add too much moisture and can be used during vegetative growth. They are very efficient. However they create too much moisture for the flowering stage.

- If there is a big drop in temperature at night many of the heat problems may be solved by running the garden lights at night, rather than during the day.

- If the plants are being grown hydroponically the water can be cooled. This keeps the entire plant cool even though the air is hot. If the room temperature is in the 80°s F (27-30 °C), keep the water temperature in the 60°s (15-20° C). Aquarium water chillers can be installed in the system to cool the water as it passes through the line.

- Remove all heat producing equipment from the growroom if possible, especially light ballasts and large pumps.

- The best way to deal with heat is to prevent it from getting into the garden to begin with. Using air or water cooled lights keeps the heat generated by the lamps from entering the garden. Tubes carry it from the lamps to the outside without affecting room air temperature.

HERMAPHRODITES

Problem: I have a plant that grew fine outside. I took cuttings and grew the plants indoors. Unlike the outdoor plant, the indoor plant turned hermaphroditic. How can I prevent this?

Solution: The plant is adapted to outdoor conditions. Growing indoors produces stress and the plant turns hermaphroditic. We know no solutions to this. Clones from plants grown indoors may exhibit hermaphrodite tendencies as part of an intergenerational non-genetic, but chromosomal, adaptation process.

Problem: I am growing six varieties in my outdoor garden, which I started from stash seeds. Three of the plants are hermaphroditic. Why? What should I do about it?

Solution: The hermaphroditic plants may be genetically programmed to be that way. That's how you got the stash seeds in the first place; the buds were self-fertilized and produced the seeds you planted.

Hermaphrodite. *Photos: Anonymous*

You could try picking the male flowers but that can be a time-consuming and is usually only partially successful, since it is so easy to miss a few flowers. If the plants are heavily laden with male flowers, removing the plants might be the best way to ensure that the other plants remain seed-free.

In the future use seeds that have a known heritage.

Problem: I have a hermaphroditic plant. She didn't have any male flowers until the third week of flowering, and they are all on an occasional branch, not interspersed. If I use the pollen from this plant to produce seed, will they be hermaphroditic?

Solution: Most of the plants resulting from the plant crossing itself will be hermaphroditic. At least some of the plants from outcrosses of the pollen or by importing pollen to cross with the hermaphrodite will produce some hermaphrodites. To simplify your life this plant should not be used for reproductive purposes.

KNOCKED DOWN PLANT

Problem: The plant was knocked down during a storm or by animals.

Solution: The plant must be picked up, supported and tied up to keep it upright. First make all the preparations. Position the support stakes, have the rope or tape ready. Gently lift the plant into position and hold it steady as it is tied up. Three or four stakes spaced around the plant or stem provide greater support than a single stake tied to the stem. With a single stake, more stress is placed on the stem-plant joint, sometimes resulting in stem breaks.

If appropriate, such as after a dry windstorm, water the plant.

If the roots were torn from the earth cover them by adding more planting medium and gently packing it around. Make sure all the roots are well covered by a thick layer of soil so they are protected from the air. Water using Super-Thrive or a B-12 rooting compound and use humic acid to help with the roots' trauma.

Sometimes it is unfeasible to raise the plant upright because of damage to the stem and branches. Still, the plant branches should be raised off the ground using shipping pallets or sawhorses. Plastic netting can be used to help support them.

Once the plant dries out and has been stabilized, usually a few days, it can be washed free of dirt using a gentle water spray. This should be done only on a warm sunny day early enough so the plant will dry completely by nightfall. Don't do this on cool or cloudy days because the moisture promotes mold growth. Place a rug under the plant to protect the buds from debris and mud.

LIGHT

Plants use light as energy. Chloroplasts, which are special organs inside leaf cells capture the red and blue spectrum waves and use them to power photosynthesis. In this process plants take elements from water and air and make sugar, while releasing free oxygen. Sugar is used to fuel metabolism, the process of living, and to build tissue, including flowers. The more light the plants have the faster the chloroplasts can function. As long as the plant is supplied with enough water, CO_2 and nutrients it increases production when it receives more light. This results in faster growth and larger yield.

Outdoors, plants thrive in full sun. Indoors, for full tight buds indicas need at least 40 watts of HPS or MH light per square foot. Sativas need at least 60 watts. MH or HPS lamps can be used for vegetative growth. HPS promotes flower growth during flowering. Fluorescents can be used for vegetative growth or for flowering. Use cool white during veg and warm whites during flowering.

NO FLOWERS

Symptom: Plants won't flower indoors.

Solution: Indoors, marijuana plants are induced to flower when the uninterrupted dark period lasts 12 hours for 4 or 5 days. After that most varieties require a continuation of that regimen. The light deprivation should start and end at the same time each day. For this reason the lights should be set on a timer and not depend on human reliability. See also Forcing Flowering.

DARK CYCLE INTERRUPTED

Problem: The lights were left on for one or more days.

Symptoms: If it happens for only a day there won't be much effect. However, if the lights are left on for several days the plants may start reverting to vegetative growth during early stages of flowering. It has less effect as the buds get closer to maturity.

Solution: Return the garden to its usual cycle immediately. This will prevent any further damage. If there has been any reversion to vegetative growth the buds will take a little longer to mature.

Problem: The lights were left off for one or more days.

Symptoms: Bud ripening may be hastened.

Solution: Turn the lights back on and maintain the regular flowering schedule until they are ripe.

Problem: The lights were turned on and off at irregular times

Symptoms: Lanky, irregular bud growth. Hermaphroditism also occurs in some cases. See Hermaphroditism for more information.

Solution: Start using a timer to keep a strict light regimen and help the buds grow and gain potency.

LIGHT BURN

See *High Temperatures: Tip Burn.*

NUTRIENT BURN

Symptom: Very deep green leaves indicate an overabundance of Nitrogen. Tip burn may indicate too much Potassium. Severe over-fertizilation results in wilting.

Solution: Stop fertilizing. Flush medium with pH-adjusted non-fertilized water.

Nutrient burn. *Photos: (left) Smknvtec, (right) The King of New York*

Sometimes plants appear to be suffering from a nutrient deficiency but treatment fails to solve the problem. It could be an excess of nutrients. This creates chemical reactions that lock up nutrients, making them insoluble and preventing them from being absorbed by the roots. When this occurs flush the plant with twice the amount of water as the size of the container.

No two nutrient burns are alike; they have different symptoms and mimic different problems. If you have added nutrients and the problems persist, flush the containers and lower the nutrient concentration. Feed plants according to their size. Large plants use more nutrients than smaller ones.

It is always best to dilute fertilizer solutions and gradually increase concentrations. If you add too much you may have to flush.

Nutrient burn. *Photo: Hansi*

PRUNING: BRANCHES

Problem: Should I prune my plants? How?

Solution: Pruning plants increases yield and decreases height while helping the stem to grow stronger and stouter. The center bud, which is the tallest part of the plant, produces auxin, a chemical that inhibits growth of other buds. When the top bud is cut, the side buds that surround the top bud start to grow vigorously. As a result, instead of growing one jumbo and several medium sized buds, several very large buds develop. They weigh more in total than the unpruned buds.

Indoors, the best time to prune is about 10 to 15 days before the plants are forced to flower. Outdoors it should be done several weeks before the plants are expected to flower. To tip the plant, cut off the new growth on the central branch near the top.

Sometimes it is more convenient to have a bushy plant with small or medium sized buds than one with fewer, larger buds. To produce a plant that looks bushy cut the top growth after the plant develops about five sets of leaves. The plant will develop four or more large side branches to replace the center growth. When these branches have developed four or five sets of leaves prune off the top growth of each branch. The plant develops numerous branches as a result.

PRUNING: LEAVES

Problem: Should the fan leaves be pruned from plants? If so, when?

Solution: Leaves are sugar factories. Specialized organs in leaf cells use the energy from light to combine carbon dioxide and oxygen to make sugar and release oxygen to the environment. The sugar is used to fuel the plant's metabolism and as a building block for new tissue. The plant spends energy to grow the leaf. Once it is grown, a leaf is a net energy generator. When leaves are picked the plant is deprived of an energy generator and does not grow as quickly as when it is left unpruned. For this reason leaves should not be pruned from plants in vegetative growth and early stages of flowering.

There are only a few stages when leaves should be removed. The first is in mid-to-late flowering. When a leaf covers or hides a bud from light, especially direct sunlight, it should manipulated into another position if possible but, if not, it should be removed. It is more important that the growing buds get light than the leaf produce sugars.

As the flowers mature and the plant is using flowering formula nutrients, which contain little or no nitrogen, the plant transfers it from the leaves to the buds. The leaves turn yellow and are of little use to the plant. They snap from the stem with the slightest pressure.

The last stage when leaves should be removed is during manicuring.

SEED GERMINATION

Problem: How do I germinate seeds?

Solution: To hasten germination and kill infectious agents soak the seed for 12 hours in a 1% hydrogen peroxide or compost tea solution. Place the seeds in sterile planting mix, pasteurized soil, planting pellets, rock wool or Oasis® cubes about one quarter inch deep. Water using a ½% hydrogen peroxide solution with bloom fertilizer added at one quarter strength. Keep the medium moist. To ensure constant humidity cover with a dome and keep out of the sun. Keep the medium at about 72°F (22°C). The seeds should germinate in 2 to 10 days. Old seeds take longer to germinate than younger ones. Keep a strong light on the seedlings or they will stretch.

Outdoors, the seeds should be planted at about the same time corn is planted by gardeners in your area. The season can be hastened using row covers but this may cause vegetative growth/flowering problems if a critical dark period is involved. This sometimes occurs when plants are placed outdoors early in the season.

The seeds should be planted about 1/4 inch (6 mm) deep on tilled soil or drilled into untilled soil. They require protection from overgrowing weeds. Once they reach unobstructed sunlight they will soon dominate the canopy.

Symptom: Do feminized seeds work? Do they produce all female plants or hermaphrodites?

Solution: All-female seeds do work. They are produced by inducing male flowers in female plants using chemicals or environmental techniques. They eliminate the need for sexing.

Gardeners report that sometimes some of the plants are hermaphroditic. This is the result of the technique that is used to produce them. When breeders use induced hermaphrodites in their breeding programs, rather than just for the last cross, they inadvertently select for hermaphroditism. Choose seeds from companies that enjoy a good reputation for these seeds.

SHORT GROWING SEASON

Symptom: The plants I want to grow won't mature in time where I live.

Symptom: Immature buds at harvest.

Solutions: Grow a different variety that does mature in time. Alternatively, force flowering early by covering the plants each day so they receive 12 hours of darkness. For instance, if you start covering the plants July 20, varieties that take eight weeks to ripen will be ready to pick by Sept 15. Starting forcing on June 20 results in ripe buds August 15.

SMALL PLANTS NOT GROWING

Symptom: The garden has bright light, is watered regularly and is being fertilized as directed, but the plant leaves are very dark colored and the plants grow very slowly.

Solution: If the plants are receiving adequate amounts of light, nutrients and water, the pH is probably out of range. This prevents the plants from utilizing the nutrients. Without nutrients the plant cannot make use of the light to create sugars for growth.

Solve the problem by adjusting the pH of the nutrient water solution to the range of 6.0-6.4. The easiest way to do this is by using pH Up or Down. These are very acid or alkaline powders and solutions and very little is required to affect water pH. Hydrated and liquified lime also work well in planting mediums.

STRETCHING

Symptom: Plants with stems that stretch are problematic in the grow room and in outdoor gardens when height is an issue.

Solution: There are several reasons why plants stretch. The first is that they are genetically programmed to grow long stems between leaf sets. Sativa varieties that grow tall outside also grow long stems indoors. Genetics aside, there are a few things that a gardener can do to shorten the stem length between the leaves.

Plants growing in a space with strong air circulation that creates stem and leaf movement strengthens and widens the stem as it slows vertical growth. When the wind bends the stem it creates tiny tears in the tissue. The plant quickly repairs these tears by

Elongated Seedlings. *Photo: Ed Rosenthal*

growing new tissue. Brushing and bending the plant leaves and stem a couple of times a day also helps widen the stem.

The light spectrum can help control height. Blue light promotes shorter, stouter stems. Red and orange light promote longer thinner stems. During vegetative growth plants grown under metal halide lamps have shorter stems than plants grown under high pressure sodium lamps.

Another light spectrum, infrared light, which is invisible to the human eye, can be used to keep height in check. It is used after the lights are turned off. Infrared light is produced by heat lamps, which also produce some red light. Placing a black cotton cloth

Elongated Seedlings. *Photos: Freezerboy (left), MoeBudz420 (right)*

Elongated Seedlings. *Photo: Ed Rosenthal*

over the heat lamp reflector allows the infrared rays to go through but captures the red light that would neutralize the effects of the invisible rays. However, this spectrum also promotes flowering and should only be used during flowering.

Heat affects stem growth, too. Plants grow longer stems as the temperature rises. At about 60°F (15°C) plants' growth slows, but the stems tend to be thicker. At 80°F (27°C) plants start to stretch. Both buds and lower stems are affected.

Sometimes buds that are close to a light grow airy or lanky. Growers erroneously attribute this to "light burn." However, this is not the problem. The difficulty is that the heat produced by the lamp is creating a very hot environment in the bud zone. There are several solutions to heat problems including using air-cooled lamps, which prevent much of the heat from entering the room. Water-cooled lamps keep almost all of the lamp heat so that plants can be placed very close to the buds without burning.

Temperature inversion is a method used in commercial greenhouses. When the temperature is higher during the dark period than the lighted period, vertical stem growth slows resulting in stronger, thicker stems. Keeping the lit temperature in the low 70's F (21-23°C) and increasing the temperature to 80°F (27°C) degrees at night slows vertical growth but does not affect yield adversely.

Lack of light causes stem elongation. Under low light conditions seedlings grow long thin stems attempting to reach more light. To stop stem stretch provide a more intense light or place the seedlings closer to the source. If they have already stretched support them using wooden skewers. Once they are given brighter light the stems fill out and they are able to support themselves. Older plants suffering from light deprivation stretch towards the light. Buds grow airy, don't tighten up and have sparse trichome coverage. Provide more light, either by adding additional bulbs or by placing the light closer to the plants.

Pruning can be used to shorten stem length. Removing the top of the main stem forces growth of the surrounding branches. These branches do not grow as long or as tall as the main stem. Bending the top branch until it breaks and hangs low also spurs lower stem growth.

TEMPERATURE

LOW TEMPERATURE

Indoors, marijuana prefers a moderate temperature: between 70-75°F (21 to 23°C) during the lit period and a temperature drop of no more than 15°F (9°C) to 60°F (15°C) at the lowest during the dark period. Plants enriched with CO_2 will yield more at a slightly higher temperature: just below 80°F (27°C).

When temperatures drop below 60°F (15°C) during the dark period plant growth slows and yields suffer. This may not be noticeable if you aren't familiar with the garden's usual yield. Cool temperature for a few nights won't make too much of a difference, but if it happens throughout the flowering period it can be a serious problem.

Solutions: Use a CO_2 generator or an electric heater to heat the room.

If the floor can be kept warm, at 80°F (27°C), the roots will be heated and the stems and leaves will be able to withstand cold air. If you have only a few plants use a plant heating mat. Larger gardens can be heated using a recirculating hot water heater.

Outdoors, most varieties can withstand temperature as low as 50°F (10°C) without problems. Fifty degrees is not an ideal temperature, since it slows growth of tissue built using sugars produced during the day and slows down photosynthesis and tissue growth when it occurs during the day. Temperatures below 40°F (4°C) often result in tissue damage.

Solutions: Gas patio heaters can keep the plants in a garden warm on chilly nights. Keeping the temperature at 60 degrees increases plant growth.

Outdoors, a sheet of polyethylene plastic secured over a simple frame keeps the temperature up and protects the garden from wind and rain. A heater provides even more protection.

HIGH TEMPERATURE

Symptom: Elongated Stems and Airy Roots

Plants can withstand high temperature as long as they have a large root system that can draw up enough water to keep the plant cool through transpiration. During vegetative growth temperatures in the 80°s and 90°s F (27-37°C) result in stem elongation. During

Heat burn. *Photos: SmknVtec*

ering it results in airy buds. This occurs both indoors and out.

Solutions: Indoors, the temperature can be lowered using ventilation, air-conditioning, or by eliminating heat from the garden using air or water-cooled lights. Remember the air temperature in the aisles of a room isn't important; it's the temperature under the lights, at the plant canopy level, that affects the plants.

Outdoors, cool the air using micro-sprayers that lower the temperature 20 to 30 degrees during day. They emit a spray with droplets that are 5 microns or smaller. The droplets evaporate, cooling the ambient air by 20 to 30 degrees.

Symptom: Wilting Plants in the Afternoon

Plants outdoors in small pots or small planting holes surrounded by bad soil have a hard time even when the soil is kept moist. This is because they don't have enough roots to draw water to the leaves. If they are in containers they may also be overheated each day as their black planting containers absorb light energy and transform it into heat.

Solutions: Check to see if the plant is root-bound. If it is then transplant it to a larger container. If the containers are dark colored paint or cover them so they are light colored and reflect most of the light.

Symptom: Tip Burn.

Symptom: The buds closest to the lights are stretching and look bleached.

Solutions: The space near the lights is too hot. This effect is sometimes mis-diagnosed as too bright a light. The buds can take the intense light: it's the heat that affects them.

In the short run, keep the lights further away from the plants.

Install air cooled lights with reflectors to reduce the heat near the light.

Water-cooled lights are extremely effective at stopping light generated heat from getting into the room.

Generally speaking 1000-watt lights should be kept about 3 feet (1 meter) from the plant tops. With air-cooling lights can be spaced 18-24 inches (45-60 cm) away. With water-cooled lights they can be placed 12 inches (30 cm) or less from the tops.

Lights can be moved closer if they are placed on light movers. Temperature changed from cold to warm, cold nights and warm days.

WATER

WHEN TO WATER

Marijuana roots should never dry out. When they do the plant wilts. When the plants are in soil or planting mix water when the medium feels as though it is losing its moisture. Waiting for it to dry out before watering, even if the plant does not show signs of wilting, deprives the plant of water it would use for growth.

The amount of water that a plant needs and how often it should be watered depend on its size, the size of the container, canopy, root level and room temperature, humidity and the stage of growth.

- Larger plants require more water.
- Larger containers need to be watered less frequently.

Symptoms of overwatering. *Photo: ShopVac*

- When the temperature is warmer plants require more water.
- When the humidity is higher plants need to be watered less frequently.
- During the last few weeks of flowering plants use less water.

Outdoors, during the hot days of summer, soils often dry out quickly and may need to be watered quite a bit. Adding compost and water-holding crystals to the soil at planting time can help it hold water for longer periods.

Covering the soil with mulch slows water evaporation dramatically. Compost, wood chips, hay or dried leaves, newspapers and even rugs can be used.

DROWNING ROOTS

Symptoms: No discoloration. Drooping, but not wilted, leaves and an unhealthy fatigued look. Very slow, if any, growth.

The Problem: When plants suffer from over watering an anaerobic condition, when there is no oxygen, is created. Roots don't use carbon dioxide, but they do use oxygen. They obtain it from the air spaces between the soil particles. When they are deprived of oxygen they cannot function properly, and gradually lose their vigor. The roots are easily attacked by pathogens.

Indoor Problems

There are three possible causes of drowning roots indoors.

- You are watering too often and the planting mix is not getting a chance to drain.
- There are no drainage holes in the bottom of the container or they are clogged.
- The soil or planting mix's particles are too small and don't have enough air spaces between them. To test this, water the mix. Once it is saturated, it should drain freely. Mixes that drain slowly have too tight a texture.

Solutions: Make sure the container has working drainage holes. If not, cut some into the container using a knife, drill or thermal tool.

If the planting mix has fine particles, water less frequently. Use a coarser, more aerated planting mix if you are transplanting and with future crops.

Outdoor Problems

Outdoors, clay and rain saturated soils are the usual causes of poor drainage. Sandy soils, on the other hand, may drain too well.

SOIL

CLAY SOILS

Problem: Clay soils are notorious for drainage problems. They form a virtually non-porous layer so the water just puddles. This creates an anaerobic condition that damages the roots.

Solution: Before planting, the clay should be dug up. Soils that are composed of clay but with substantial amounts of other materials can be modified using compost, fresh organic matter, sand, perlite, or used planting mix. Gypsum and sulfur are sometimes used to modify clay chemically. They both act to break up its tight molecular structure.

Soils that are almost all clay are very difficult to garden. Alternatives are creating a raised bed or using a large container to hold soil above ground, or excavating the clay and replacing it with different soil. If you are digging planting holes try to reach a permeable layer. You might use an auger bit on a drill to create a drainage hole that reaches a permeable layer. If you know that an area will be saturated from rain during the growing season build mounds or raised beds to keep the roots comfortably above the water level.

SANDY SOILS

Sandy soils don't hold water. Instead it drains, quickly leaving the plants thirsty if water isn't supplied quite often, sometimes even several times a day. To increase the soil's water-holding qualities add compost and other decayed plant matter. This may require moving a lot of material and may not be feasible. Water-holding crystals also help.

Irrigate over a period of time using small amounts of water such as a drip. This way the ground is kept evenly moist. When it is watered all at once, it drains and after a short time the soil is moisture deficient. One simple solution is to use a 2½ gallon (9.5 Liter) water container that has an adjustable spigot or a larger container. Adjust it to a steady drip, so it drips the whole day. Those steady drops will keep the plant from getting thirsty. Re-fill the container when it is empty.

Example of wilting plant against a healthy plant. *Photo: Anonymous*

Another solution is to dig a planting hole 18 inches (45 cm) deep. Put a 3-6 inch (7-15 cm) deep plastic tray or a heavy duty plastic bag at the bottom of the hole and fill it up with the soil. The tray or bag will act as an underground reservoir and keep water from draining too quickly.

DRIED-OUT SOIL

Add a wetting agent to the water to prevent it from beading on the surface of the soil. Wetting agents allow water to be easily absorbed into the soil, and are available at garden shops. Gardeners sometimes use soap or detergents as wetting agents.

UNDER-WATERING: WILTED PLANTS

Symptom: Plants grow slowly, wilting.

Solution: Water the plants. If they are wilted do not use fertilizer-enriched water. Use un-enriched, but pH-adjusted water. After they have perked up you can re-institute the fertilizer program.

If the amount of water is just barely adequate to maintain the plants, growth slows down. This may be hard to notice. However once the plants receive more generous supplies of water, provided they have enough nutrients, they will experience a growth spurt.

CHLORINE IN WATER

Problem: The irrigation water has large amounts of chlorine. Does this have a bad effect on the plants?

Solution: Chlorine affects plants in several ways. First, in media systems it kills some of the microorganisms that form a community with the roots in the rhizosphere. This results in slower growth. Some leaf tip burn may be the result of excess chlorine. This is most likely to happen during hot sunny days when the plant uses a lot of water.

Most gardeners water straight from the tap, which most likely has been treated with chlorine and possibly fluoride. In spite of these chemicals in the water plants grow well. They may grow better with non-chlorinated water. Most city water is chlorinated with chloramines, which cannot be removed by boiling or allowing the water to stand. If you wish to dechlorinate tap water, activated carbon filters will do the job. There are also specialized UV systems designed specifically for dechlorination. A number of chemical dechlorinators are available for use in fish ponds and aquariums. These products are safe for fish and plants, however the author has not tried them and cannot say for certain which works best in marijuana gardens.

HARD OR SOFT WATER

Symptoms: Erratic deficiencies and growth problems.

Solution: Check water for dissolved solids. It should be between 100-150 parts per million (ppm). Water that is too low (soft water) should be adjusted to 150 ppm using Cal-Mag solution. Water that is too high, with over 250 ppm dissolved solids, should be filtered using ionic or reverse osmosis filters .

Hard water prevents balanced nutrient uptake. Filtered water can be mixed with unfiltered to create water suitable for plants. Water in a Los Angeles suburb measured 450 ppm dissolved solids. After filtering through an ionic filter it had a ppm of 13. The gardener mixed one part of unfiltered water to two parts filtered resulting in a solids level in the mixed water of just above 150 ppm. The water has the right amount of dissolved solids for use in a nutrient water solution.

Hard water deposits can damage hydroponic/aeroponic systems.

SODIUM IN WATER

Avoid any water that contains high levels of sodium. Sodium is absorbed by the plant first before any other element. It causes the plant's vascular system to break down. Water treated with water softeners should be avoided.

SULFUR IN WATER

Water with a sulfurous odor should be checked for its pH. Sulfur is acidic and the water may have a very low pH. Adjust the pH of the water with pH Up. Soils that have been irrigated with the water may also be affected and have a low pH, indicating acidity. These soils should also be tested and adjusted if necessary using lime, which raises the pH.

WATER TEMPERATURE

Problem: What temperature should I keep my hydroponic water?

Solution: In a garden with a canopy at normal temperature of no higher than 78ºF (24ºC) keep the water at about 72-74ºF (22-23ºC). If the canopy temperature is higher then lower the water temperature a few degrees.

WEATHER
COLD SPELLS

Problem: The weather report says that we are going to experience a cold spell that will dip below freezing. This is to be followed by warmer weather later in the month. How do I prepare my garden for the cold?

Solution: The idea here is to keep the plants alive until the weather changes. If the temperature can be kept at 45ºF (7ºC) or more the plants will survive unscathed. Then when better weather returns they will start growing again.

If the plants can be moved inside and given moderate light on cycle they can be preserved for a few days until the outside weather changes.

A patio heater can be placed in the garden and may provide enough heat to keep the plant from frostbite. A temporary greenhouse constructed of wood frame and plastic will preserve the heat better and can be removed when better weather arrives.

Individual plants can be wrapped using polyethylene. This protects the plants from wind and preserves some heat. However, the cold will eventually get to the plants unless there is some source of heat for them. Forced air heaters can deliver heat to the plants. Make sure to set the gauge at about 70°F (21°C) so the plants do not overheat.

COOL WEATHER

Problem: The plants are not mature and the weather is getting cooler. How long can the plants stay outside?

Solution: Plant growth slows dramatically as the daylight temperature slips down into the low 60°s F (15-18°C) and virtually stops in the mid-50°s (12-14°C). If it is unlikely that the temperature will rise to the high 60° or 70°s F (above 20°C) then it may be useless to keep the plants growing.

At the same time the evening temperature may be slipping dangerously low. The plants can withstand temperatures in the 40°s F (5-10°C) but when it slips into the 30°s (below 4°C), tissue damage is likely.

The solution depends on the amount of sunlight available. As autumn turns closer to winter the intensity of sunlight diminishes tremendously and its light reaches earth at a lower (more oblique) angle. Often plants that were in full light during summer and early autumn are shaded most of the time. Clouds may obscure the sun most of the time. The plants do not receive enough light energy to support growth. They should be harvested. If the buds are too immature to smoke they can be processed for kief, extracts or for cooking.

If the plants are getting sunlight but are still experiencing cold weather they could be protected using clear plastic hanging over a frame. The air inside the frame heats up, so growth is promoted.

One way to keep the air warm at night in enclosed spaces is to use passive heaters made by filling dark-colored containers with water. The containers heat up during the day, then radiate heat at night.

Patio heaters that use propane tanks can also be used to keep the plants warm. Burning the gas produces CO_2 and water vapor. The extra CO_2 promotes plant growth.

HUMID WEATHER

Problem: The weather is turning humid.

Solution: Harvest all mature buds. Spray the plants with anti-fungals. Keep the plants on the warm side if possible.

If this weather is common during the ripening season then plant varieties with looser buds that dry out more easily.

RAINY WEATHER

Problem: Rainy weather is forecast. How can the plants be protected?

Solution: Rainy weather promotes mold. Water gets into the buds and creates a perfect environment for molds such as Botrytis to grow. The buds hold the water and humidity in their crevices so it is hard to dry them out.

If the plants can be moved or a protective enclosure can be constructed the plants will be protected from rain, but not moisture. Raising the temperature of the enclosed area into the high 70s (24-26ºC), beyond the optimal range for mold growth, may protect the plants and help dry out the buds. A fan circulating the hot air helps.

If the rain is expected to be brief followed by warming dry weather the plants can be protected by treating the plants with one of the anti-fungals such as potassium bicarbonate or Serenade® before the rain starts. If the forecast is for prolonged rain, the best solution may be to harvest the plants rather than risk them turning to mush.

WILTING

Problem: Wilting appears suddenly. One moment the plants are fine and a few minutes later wilting starts that can progress slowly or quickly.

Solution: Plants draw water up by keeping a higher salt concentration in their tissues than in the surrounding soil. If the salts (fertilizer nutrients) become more concentrated in the planting mix than the plant, either the plant can no longer draw up water or it actually drains from the plant. Use pH adjusted 72ºF (22ºC) degree water to flush the soil. Use water equal to about one and a half times the volume of the container, or about 7 gallons of water to flush a five-gallon container.

Cannabis leaves sometimes droop right at the end of the light period; this is not a cause for concern.

ORGANIC AND IPM CONTROL

Here you can find a description of many of the control methods previously listed in this book. You will be re-informed as to whether the control is used to battle nutrient deficiencies, pests or diseases and be given specific instruction on how to use each control.

All of these are safe to use for herb or for edible crops. Sprays are washed away by water, including rain, so plan to reapply spray products after rain or any watering that hits the affected areas of the plants.

A GENERAL NOTE ON CONTROL PRODUCTS

Always read the label carefully before buying or using any control product. You need to follow the manufacturer's directions carefully to use these products safely and avoid harming the plants. You also need to identify the ingredients in a product to be sure that it will treat the problem you're dealing with, and will not introduce additional problems you don't want. Many modern garden products seek to be all-in-one cures for common garden problems, for example, a micronutrient fertilizer that also contains high levels of nitrogen. Others apply more than one control for the same problem, such as a pyrethrum product that also contains rotenone or piperonyl butoxide. If that's what you need for your situation, fine, but check the label to avoid surprises.

If you are applying any product that you have never used before, including a new home-made recipe, always test it on a few branches of a plant and wait a day or two before applying it to your entire garden.

ALFALFA AND COTTONSEED MEAL

These are granulated products made from pressed alfalfa hay and the solids remaining after cotton seeds are pressed for oil. Both are high in protein and are used as animal feeds. Because of their high protein content they are also high in nitrogen, and can be added to soil or planting mix as slow-release nitrogen fertilizers.

Look for alfalfa and cottonseed meals at farm animal feed stores and garden centers under many different brands.

AMPELOMYCES QUISQUALIS

This is a beneficial fungus available commercially under the brand name AQ-10®. It is effective against powdery mildew.

ANT BAITS

These products contain a poison such as boric acid, arsenic or sulfluramid and an attractive bait that entices the ants to carry it back to their nest, where it kills both workers and queens. Available in many brands, including Grants Ant Stakes, Terro Liquid Borate Ant Bait, Enforcer Ant Bait, Advance® Dual-Choice Bait Station and Drax Liquidator® Ant Bait Station.

APHID MIDGES

Aphidoletes aphidimyza is a small fly (2 to 3 mm long) that looks a little like a mosquito. The larvae are bright orange and are attracted to the smell of honeydew. They attack and consume aphids by the score.

Buy them as pupae from companies such as Buglogical, Planet Natural, Hydro-Gardens, Natural Insect Control, Peaceful Valley and EcoSolutions. The pupae hatch into adults, which lay eggs and produce the aphid-destroying larvae. Plan on using about 100 pupae per 100 square feet.

BACILLUS PUMILUS

Bacillus pumilus is a naturally occurring bacterium that produces compounds that kills active fungal infections and inhibits further growth. Strain QST 2808 of this bacterium has been patented for use as a biorational fungicide against Fusarium, gray mold and powdery mildew, under the brand name Sonata®. It is most effective when applied as a preventive measure before symptoms appear.

Sonata® is effective for about 10 days after each application. I found that it does not completely eliminate powdery mildew when used alone but it does work very well in conjunction with *Bacillus subtilis* fungicides such as Serenade®.

BACILLUS SUBTILIS

Bacillus subtilis is another naturally occurring fungicidal bacterium. Several strains of this bacterium have been patented for use against gray mold, powdery mildew, Verticillium, Pythium and Fusarium, under brand names such as Serenade®, Rhizopro® and Subtilex®. It is most effective when applied as a preventive measure before symptoms appear.

B. subtilis fungicides are considered totally safe to humans and animals since the bacteria attack only fungi. It is easy to use and quite effective. Used weekly, it puts powdery mildew into remission.

BACILLUS THURINGIENSIS

Bacillus thuringiensis is a naturally occurring bacterium that is lethal to caterpillars and fungus gnat larvae. Commercial brands include Dipel®, Javelin®, Thuricide®, Vectobac®, Teknar®, XanTari® and Gnatrol®. Note that various strains of *B. thuringiensis* are effective against different pests, so check the label to verify that the product you're buying controls the problem you're having. In addition to killing off existing pests it also prevents infestation or re-infestation.

BARLEY STRAW RAFTS & PELLETS

Barley straw rafts floating in the water are algaecidal. They are useful in hydroponic systems and reservoirs. This effect is due to hydrogen peroxide produced by a complex series of chemical reactions as the barley decays.

BEAUVERIA BASSIANA (BENEFICIAL FUNGI)

B. bassiana is a fungus that attacks and kills a variety of pests, including whiteflies, leaf miners, aphids, spider mites and caterpillars. Note that many beneficial insects, such as lady beetles, are also susceptible. Products containing Beauveria work by contact, but take three to seven days to germinate, penetrate and kill target pests. Spray plants thoroughly as soon as you identify an infestation. In addition to killing off existing pests it also prevents infestation or re-infestation.

Commercial products containing *B. bassiana* include Naturalis H&G®, Mycotrol® and Botanigard®.

BORIC ACID

Boric Acid is one of the best cures for boron deficiencies as well as a common, safe and effective ant poison. It is also effective against termites and cockroaches. It can be sprinkled as a powder or laid down as a barrier wherever pests are seen, but it is usually more effective laced into a bait. Many commercial baits are available, including Drax®, Ant Kil Gel, Borid®, and Dr. Moss® Liquid Ant Bait. However you can make your own using recipes like these:

Sugar Bait Grease Bait

Sugar (1 cup)

Boric Acid (4 teaspoons)

Water (3 cups)   Canned cat food (about 1 cup)

Boric acid (1 tablespoon)

Mix ingredients and put small amounts of the solution or cat food mixture in shallow dishes near plants. Keep these baits out of reach of pets and children.

CAL-MAG

These are nutrient supplements that contain both calcium and magnesium, suitable for correcting deficiencies in either or both of these minerals. Brands include Botanicare® Cal-Mag Plus®, Sensi-Cal®, MagiCal® and Cal-Max®.

Note that different Cal-Mag products contain different levels of nitrogen, phosphorous, and potassium, the big three macronutrients. Check the label on the product you're thinking of using, and avoid using high-nitrogen products during flowering or high-phosphorous products during vegetative growth.

CALCIUM NITRATE

Various compounds such as calcium nitrate ($CaNO_3$) and calcium acetate ($CaCH_3CO_2$) are used to correct calcium deficiencies. Calcium nitrate is especially useful as it provides both calcium and nitrogen in readily available forms. It is available at larger garden centers under the Viking fertilizer brand, and through scientific supply houses under brand names such as Aldrich and Sigma.

Beware of using calcium nitrate during the flowering stage because it will provide more nitrogen than the plant should have at that stage of growth.

CAPSAICIN

This is the substance that gives hot peppers their heat. Pepper plants produce capsaicin for its repellent value against insects and other animals that might otherwise eat the plants. It provides similar protection when applied to other plants.

Cayenne pepper contains capsaicin, and it can be sprinkled as a powder to repel ants. You can also make an insecticidal pepper spray with this recipe:

1/2 ounce (15 g) dried or 4 ounces (60 g) fresh peppers (habanero or other very hot pepper)

2 tablespoons (30 mL) of vegetable oil

1/4 teaspoon (1 gram) lecithin granules

1/4 teaspoon (1 gram) wetting agent

Water to make up one pint (450 ml)

You can also substitute 2 tablespoons (30 mL) of Asian hot pepper oil for peppers. Wear gloves whenever you handle peppers or pepper oil, and avoid touching your eyes or mouth with your gloved hands. Grind the peppers (do not discard the seeds) and oil together in a blender. Add the water, wetting agent and lecithin and mix thoroughly. The mixture can be used immediately, but will become stronger if the peppers are allowed to soak. Strain the mixture through a cheesecloth or pantyhose into a glass jar for storage. Label the jar "Pepper Spray Concentrate." To use, mix 1 to 2 tablespoons (15-30 mL) of this concentrate with 1 pint of water and spray on plants.

As with all home recipes, test this spray on a few leaves and wait a day to check for damage, before applying it to your whole garden.

Commercial products that contain capsaicin include Hot Pepper Spray®, Bonide® Hot Pepper Wax (for ants, aphids, leaf miners, spider mites, thrips and whiteflies), Repellex® Mole, Vole and Gopher Repellent (for moles and gophers), Browseban® and Liquid Fence® (for deer).

CARBON DIOXIDE

Plants use carbon dioxide (CO_2) for photosynthesis, and it is present in the atmosphere at 300-400 ppm. Growers often use CO_2 tanks to increase the levels of this gas to 1,500-2,000 ppm in their grow rooms and greenhouses, and these levels are not harmful to most animal life. However increasing the carbon dioxide level to 10,000 ppm (1%) and holding it at that level for an hour kills most insects, including spider mites, whiteflies, aphids and thrips. Take care to vent the room thoroughly after this treatment, as such high levels of CO_2 are hazardous for humans as well.

Carbon dioxide is also useful against ants, moles, and gophers. Against moles or gophers, drop 8 to 16 ounces (225 to 450 grams) of dry ice into the tunnel, or deliver a similar amount of CO_2 from a tank. Against ants, pour 1 gallon of seltzer water into the anthill, or inject CO_2 into the nest from a tank, using a wand.

CASTOR OIL

This is a popular ingredient in mole and gopher repellents. It repels by both taste and smell. The liquid can be smeared on paper and dropped into the gopher's burrow. Commercial repellents such as Repellex® Mole, Vole and Gopher Repellent, Molemax® and Sweeney's® Mole & Gopher Repellent may be easier to use.

CHELATED MINERALS

Chelation is a chemical process whereby nutrient minerals (such as magnesium, boron, copper, iron, manganese, zinc and others) are made more available to plants by combining them with a compound such as citric acid or EDTA (ethylenediamine tetraacetic acid). Many hydroponic micronutrient formulas contain a blend of chelated minerals. Other products contain single metal chelates for treating specific deficiencies. Brands depend on the specific mineral of interest:

Copper: Librel™ Copper Chelate, YEOMAN® 5% Cu

Iron: Bonide Liquid Iron (also contains Zn and Mn), Plant-Prod® Iron Chelate

Manganese: Growth Product Manganese Chelate, Librel™ Manganese Chelate

Zinc: YEOMAN® 7% Zn, Nulex® Liquid Zinc

CHOLECALCIFEROL (VITAMIN D3)

This is one of the more modern rat poisons, developed because it is significantly less toxic to humans than it is to rats and mice. Of course all rat poisons should be treated with care, and deployed only in tamper-proof bait stations. Commercial baits such as Quintox® and Campaign® are effective.

CINNAMON OIL AND TEA

Cinnamon destroys powdery mildew, with an effectiveness rate of 50-70%. It doesn't eradicate mildew completely but it keeps it in check. It also potentiates other suppressive sprays so it is good to use in combination. In addition to its fungicidal properties it is effective against ants, aphids, fungus gnats, spider mites, thrips and whiteflies.

Mix food grade oil (available at herb shops) at the rate of 1 part to 200 parts water or a bit under one teaspoon (5 mL) per quart (950 mL). Or make a tea directly from cinnamon: boil water, turn off the heat and add one ounce of cinnamon to one and a half pints water. Let the tea cool to room temperature. Add half a pint of 100 proof grain alcohol or rubbing alcohol and let sit. Strain the cinnamon. The spray is ready to use. A faster method is to add 2 teaspoons (10 mL) cinnamon oil to one pint (500 mL) of water and add a dash of castile soap. Rosemary oil and wintergreen oil are also sometimes combined with cinnamon oil. The solution should consist of no more than 0.75% total oil.

Repel ants with cinnamon powder, either alone or mixed 50/50 with diatomaceous earth. Sprinkle the powder wherever you find ants entering.

Zero Tolerance® contains cinnamon oil in both its pesticide and fungicide formulations. Dr. Earth® Pro-Active™ Fruit and Vegetable Insect Spray, Cinnacure® and FlowerPharm™ are other brand name preparations.

CLOVE OIL

Clove oil is used in some botanical fungicides. Eugenol, a component of clove oil, is both a fungicide and a potent contact insecticide. It has virtually no residual activity, although the scent lingers. Eugenol is considered a minimum risk ingredient of pesticides. It has very low risk of damage to the environment or user. It is effective against Pythium, gray mold, Fusarium, ants, caterpillars, thrips, aphids and spider mites.

Zero Tolerance® contains clove oil in both its pesticide and fungicide formulations. Dr. Earth® Pro-Active™ Fruit and Vegetable Insect Spray, Phyta-Guard EC, GC-Mite®, Natura Bug-A-Tak® and Bioganic® Lawn and Garden Spray are also commercial clove oil preparations.

COMPOST & COMPOST TEA

Compost is rich black material similar to soil, produced by the controlled decomposition of organic materials (vegetable scraps, yard waste, etc.). You can buy it at garden centers, or make your own. It is a rich source of beneficial microbes and micronutrients, and provides many benefits to improve overall plant health. The beneficial microbes in compost act as barriers to infection and also destroy pathogenic organisms.

It can be worked into the soil or incorporated into a container planting mix before planting, and it can be prepared as a tea and applied by irrigation or foliar spray. Compost tea requires special care in hydroponic systems. It presents no difficulties as a foliar spray, but it should be added to the nutrient solution only in drip to drain systems, and should be thoroughly filtered before use.

Some hydroponics shops prepare compost tea on the premises, and sell it fresh. They also sell kits under brands such as SoilSoup and Vermicorp to enable the home user to make his own. To prepare your own tea you can use one of these kits, or assemble a bucket, an aquarium air pump (with hose and "bubbler" attached), a nylon stocking and enough compost to fill the bucket about 1/4 full. Buckets larger than one gallon (4 L) may require more bubblers for adequate aeration.

Load the compost into the stocking to make a "compost teabag." Tie the end of the stocking to the bucket handle and put the bag in the bucket. Some compost tea recipes call for molasses. However this encourages the growth of E. coli and other pathogenic bacteria. Fill the bucket with water and put the air hose and bubbler from the pump at the bottom of the bucket. Run the bubbler to keep the solution aerated for about a day. Switch off the pump and let the tea settle. The liquid in the bucket should be deep brown, with no unpleasant smell. A smell of ammonia or rot means that the tea has become anaerobic and should not be used as a foliar spray.

Compost tea must be used as quickly as possible because it turns anaerobic within a few hours after aeration stops. Strain the liquid through a cheesecloth strainer or filter and apply as a foliar spray or add it to your irrigation water. The used compost can be spread on the surface of the soil around the plants.

Compost and compost tea are "tonics" that promote plant health and help to prevent disease, not specific cures for any pathogen. The effectiveness of these preparations depends greatly on how they're made, but a well-made compost can do a lot to produce healthy plants.

COPPER

Copper has been used as a fungicide for centuries. When copper is dissolved in water, its ions pass through the fungus cell walls and attack proteins in the cells, killing them. It is extremely effective at destroying powdery mildew, gray mold, Septoria leaf spot, and Pythium, but can also cause injury to plant tissue. There are many commercial ready-to-use copper fungicides available, such as Kocide®, Copper-Count®-N, Cueva Fungicide, Concern® fungicidal soap and TopCop®.

Bordeaux Mixture is a mixture of hydrated lime (calcium hydroxide - $Ca(OH)_2$) and copper sulfate ($CuSO_4$) in water. It is highly effective in controlling gray mold, powdery mildew, and Septoria leaf spot. The prepared mix is available commercially under brand names such as Dexol Bordeaux fungicide and Hi-Yield Bordeaux mix. Because it is strongly basic and copper can be hazardous to humans and pets, we do not recommend Bordeaux mixture except for rampant infections. Try other sprays for smaller outbreaks.

Outdoors, copper fungicides should be used only before flowering. Indoors where the spray can be more controlled it can be used on leaf areas, but not the bud, because getting it on the bud could lead to ingestion, which does have health consequences. Don't use sprayed leaves. Throw them away.

Copper fungicides can also be applied as foliar sprays to treat copper deficiency in plants.

Copper formulas use various compounds that have different toxicity to plants. Before using any copper formula on the whole garden test it on a portion of a plant to make sure it doesn't cause injury. Apply as little copper as possible and don't apply it in cold wet weather, which increases copper ion availability and its toxicity to plants. Copper fungicides are implicated in toxicological problems of farm workers who are constant contact with them. However it has been used in home gardens and orchards for centuries with few problems. Use protective clothing when working with copper formulas.

CORIANDER OIL

This natural essential oil acts as a fungicide and insecticide to control Pythium, gray mold, Fusarium, powdery mildew, Septoria, aphids, thrips, spider mites and whiteflies. It can be purchased in a commercial blend as SM-90®.

CULTURAL CONTROLS

This category doesn't refer to social customs, but rather to ways of cultivating plants that help minimize or eliminate pests. For example, allowing the soil around plants to dry somewhat between waterings helps to control many sorts of soil-borne fungi and also reduces the population of fungus gnats. Watering in the mornings allows the soil to dry out before slugs and snails come out at night.

Growing in containers with pasteurized planting mix (either indoors or out) reduces or eliminates many soil-dwelling fungi and pests.

In outdoor gardens, maintain a favorable environment for beneficial insects and they'll do a lot of your pest control for you. Indoors, keep grow room humidity under 50% to help prevent gray mold.

Keep light out of hydroponic water systems to prevent growth of algae.

Keep your grow room clean and never bring in clothing that has just been outdoors —this helps keep out many pests.

CREAM OF TARTAR

This material is available at most grocery stores. In addition to its many cooking uses, it repels ants. To apply cream of tartar, first determine where the ants are entering. This usually means following an ant trail back to a crack or other small opening in a wall, baseboard, or window. Once the point of entry is found, sprinkle a liberal coating of cream of tartar on and around the opening.

DIATOMACEOUS EARTH

Diatoms are microscopic sea creatures with hard silica shells. The diatoms of ancient seas left large deposits of a chalky mineral that can be easily crumbled into a white powder: diatomaceous earth. This is available at most garden supply shops.

Diatomaceous earth contains microscopic fragments of glassy silica that injure and even kill small, soft-bodied animals. Kill fungus gnat larvae and thrips pupae by placing a layer about 1 inch (2.5 cm) deep atop the soil in plant pots. Deter ants, slugs and snails with a thin but unbroken barrier of diatomaceous earth about 3 inches (7 to 8 cm) wide. Mix with boric acid, ground cinnamon, or ground cloves to increase its effectiveness.

FERTILIZERS

Basic garden fertilizers are rated by their NPK numbers. These are noted on the label as a series of three numbers such as 15-5-10, 5-1-1, etc., describing the content of the three major macronutrients in the product. The first number always represents the nitrogen (N) content of the fertilizer. The number is the percent of the element in the fertilizer. The second represents the equivalent of the phosphorous compound P_2O_5. The third is the equivalent of the potassium (K) compound K_2O (potash). Thus, a fertilizer with NPK values of 10-5-1 would contain 10% nitrogen, 5% equivalent of P_2O_5 phosphate, and 1% equivalent of the potassium compound potash. For brevity's sake they are called N-P-K.

Choose a fertilizer according to the deficiency (if any) that you are trying to treat, and also to the growth stage of the plants. Nitrogen promotes vegetative growth, so it is most needed during the vegetative period. Avoid fertilizers high in nitrogen during the flowering stage. Conversely, phosphorous is most needed during flowering, and should be used with care during vegetative growth. Potassium is useful at all stages of a plant's growth, and is added to balance the pH of high-phosphorous fertilizers.

FISH EMULSION AND FISH MEAL

Whole fish deemed unsuitable for regular food use (such as menhaden), and the bones and offal from processed fish, are pressed to remove the fish oil. The remains after this pressing are a brown powder (fish meal) and a liquid emulsion (fish emulsion). Both are high in nitrogen and useful organic fertilizers (especially for treating nitrogen deficiencies). They also provide many micronutrients that help prevent deficiencies.

Fish emulsion releases nitrogen to the plant more rapidly, whereas fish meal provides a steady, slow release. Look for brands such as Alaska Fish Emulsion, Fertrell Liquid Fish Emulsion, Down To Earth Fish Meal, and Peaceful Valley Fish Meal.

FUMIGANTS

Sometimes the only way to eliminate gophers and moles is by gassing them. Several "smoke bombs" are sold for this purpose, such as Dexol Gopher Gasser and Revenge Rodent Smoke Bomb. These are thick paper cartridges filled with charcoal, sodium nitrate, and sometimes sulfur. You light the fuse and put it in the gopher's burrow. Toxic fumes from the burning cartridge do the rest.

GARLIC

Garlic is antifungal and anti-bacterial. It is used as an ingredient in fungicides and can be prepared as a spray and used every few days. Garlic has several pathways for destroying fungi including its high sulfur content. Garlic can also be added to other anti-fungal sprays.

You can make your own garlic spray from a teaspoon of garlic oil in a pint of water with 2 ounces (60 mL) of 100 proof or higher drinking alcohol such as rum or vodka. Use garlic as a preventive. Spray on new growth before there is a sign of infection.

Garlic is a general purpose insecticide as well as fungicide, so it should be used with caution on outdoor plants. It kills beneficial insects as well as plant pests. Dr. Earth Pro-Active™ Fruit and Vegetable Insect Spray, VeggiePharm, Garlic Barrier®, BioRepel and Envirepel® are garlic insecticides for ants, aphids, caterpillars, spider mites, thrips and whiteflies. Garlic fungicides are effective against powdery mildew in brands such as GC-3, Garlic GP Ornamental and Citrall Lawn and Garden Fungicide. Garlic is also an ingredient in several commercial deer repellents, such as Deer-Off® and DeerPharm.

GLIOCLADIUM (BENEFICIAL FUNGUS)

Gliocladium is a genus of soil-dwelling fungi that attack and destroy pathogenic fungi such as Pythium and Fusarium. It is best applied as a soil drench before any symptoms of infection are noticed. *Gliocladium* fungicides are sold under brands such as Gliomix®, SoilGard®, Primastop®, and Prestop®.

GRAPEFRUIT SEED EXTRACT

Grapefruit seed extract is sold as a general purpose disinfectant, and can be used to control algae in hydroponic systems. Look for brands such as Citricidal® and Nutribiotic®. Follow label instructions for control of algae, as different brands contain different concentrations of grapefruit seed extract.

GRANITE DUST

The powdered rock left over from quarrying granite (called rock dust, granite dust, or stone meal) is a good slow-release source of potassium in soil and container gardening. Depending on the source of the stone, granite dust may also contain a variety of micronutrients, which are listed on the label. It is available through garden shops under brand names such as Fishers Creek, Down To Earth and Agrowinn.

GREENSAND

Greensand is not really sand, but rather a soft, easily crumbled form of sandstone rock that is usually colored dark green. The green color comes from an iron-potassium silicate mineral called glauconite, and as you might expect greensand is a good slow-release source of potassium and iron when you don't want to introduce nitrogen as well. Greensand is also a significant source of phosphorous and contains small amounts of many other micronutrients such as copper and manganese. Brands include Fertrell® Jersey Greensand, Gardener's Supply Company Greensand and various local and store brands.

GUANO

The droppings (guano) of bats and seabirds are harvested commercially and sold as organic fertilizers. Depending on the source, guano are high in nitrogen, phosphorous, or both, and are excellent relatively available fertilizers for treating or preventing deficiencies in these nutrients. Because guano vary widely, always check the NPK value on the label to make sure that a given guano fertilizer meets your needs. Guano is available under many different brands through garden supply shops.

To make the nutrients in guano more readily available to the plants, simmer the guano in water in a slow cooker for several hours (outside, to avoid a major odor problem). Many of the nutrients will dissolve into the water and are then available for immediate uptake by the plants. If you are making a large quantity, then you may wish to prepare a concentrate to be diluted later. The solution thus made can be used either as a foliar spray or for irrigating the roots.

GYPSUM

Gypsum is a natural mineral composed of calcium sulfate ($CaSO_4$). It is useful as a slow-release form of calcium or sulfur that doesn't affect the soil pH too much. It should not be added to soils with a pH below 5.5 because it interacts with aluminum (Al) in those acidic soils, making the Al soluble and poisonous to the plants. Gypsum is available at garden centers under various local and store brands.

Gypsum can also be used to break up clay soils.

HORTICULTURAL OIL

Horticultural oils are any of a number of light oils used to control insects such as aphids, fungus gnats, leaf miners, mealybugs, scales, spider mites, thrips, and whiteflies. They work by smothering insects, and so must be applied directly to the target pests. They provide no residual activity. Some horticultural oils are vegetable-based, while others are petroleum-based. Both are effective, but if you wish to avoid petroleum products then be sure to check the label. In any case, petroleum-based oils should not be used on buds, or on leaves that you plan to use for cooking of kiefing.

These oils need to be distinguished from neem oil, which poisons pests, although, like neem oil, some horticultural oils such as jojoba, sesame and cottonseed oil have fungicidal properties. They can be used in combination with other spray ingredients listed here. The oils are mixed at about 1-2% concentrations. A 1% solution is about a teaspoon per pint (5 mL per 500 mL), 3 tablespoons per gallon (40 mL per 4 L), one quart in 25 gallons. Add a wetting agent or castile soap to help the ingredients mix.

Oil sprays should be used only on the leaves, not the buds. Use weekly on new growth. Horticultural oils are classified as "dormant" oils, which are used on plants during the winter seasons, and "summer" oils, which are used on growing plants. Summer oils tend to be lighter and more highly refined. Some oils can be used for either purpose. Marijuana gardens need only summer oils, and dormant oils can harm growing plants. So check the label on any horticultural oil you're thinking of using in your garden to verify that it is rated for use on growing plants. Some suitable brands include Dr. Earth Pro-Active™ Fruit and Vegetable Insect Spray, GC-Mite®, Organocide™, Control Solutions Ultra Fine Oil and Green Light Horticultural Oil.

HYDROGEN PEROXIDE

Hydrogen peroxide (hp, chemical formula H_2O_2) is a contact disinfectant that leaves no residue. Use it to control algae, gray mold, Pythium and powdery mildew. Hp can be used daily with no adverse effects on the plants: it produces only oxygen and water vapor as it works.

Household hp sold in drug stores has a concentration of 3%. Garden shops sell 10% hp. ZeroTol® contains 27% hydrogen dioxide and 5% peroxyacetic acid, with an activity equivalent to about 40% hp. It is considered hazardous because it can cause skin burn similar to that caused by concentrated acids.

To treat plants with drug store grade 3% hp use 4½ tablespoons (70 mL) and fill to make a pint (500 mL) of solution, or a quart of hp to 3 quarts of water.

With horticultural grade 10% hp use about 4 teaspoons per pint (20 mL per 500 mL), 10 ounces per gallon (300 mL per 4 Liters).

With ZeroTol use about 2 teaspoons per pint (10 mL per 500 mL), 5 tablespoons per gallon (75 mL per 4 Liters).

HYDROPONIC MICRONUTRIENT PRODUCTS

Hydroponic supply companies stock a variety of products that are intended to supply the many micronutrients (as opposed to nitrogen, phosphorous and potassium, the macronutrients) that plants need. They are useful for treating or preventing various micronutrient deficiencies, including copper, molybdenum and iron deficiencies. Brands include BetterGrowHydro Micro-Mix, General Hydroponics FloraMicro and Bio-Genesis® Mineral Matrix Micro-Nutrient Supplement.

Note that some micronutrient products contain macronutrient fertilizers as well. There's nothing inherently wrong with that, as long as you use a product that is balanced to provide the appropriate levels of nitrogen, phosphorous and potassium for the plants' current stage of growth. Likewise, if you're trying to treat a specific micronutrient deficiency you'll want to be sure that the product you're using contains that nutrient. Always check the labels on nutrient products to make sure you know what you're getting.

IRON PHOSPHATE

Iron phosphate is one of the best organic means of eliminating slugs and snails. Once they eat a small amount of iron phosphate the pests stop eating and soon die. It is harmless to plants and pets, unlike poisons such as metaldehyde. Iron phosphate comes in small white pellets under brand names such as Slug-go® and Escargo®. Sprinkle it liberally around your garden, as well as in shrubbery, ground cover, and other places where slugs and snails like to hide during the day.

IRON SUPPLEMENTS

Use these products to correct iron deficiencies. Most contain chelated iron, iron sulfate, or iron oxides. Brands include Glorious Gardens™ Iron Sulfate, Bonide® Iron Sulfate, Monterey Dr. Iron, Phyto-Plus® Iron 5% and Biomin® Iron.

KELP CONCENTRATES

Kelp is a family of seaweeds. Certain types can be harvested and prepared as liquid or granular plant supplements. These concentrates contain a wide range of vitamins, minerals, macro- and micronutrients. They are especially useful for treating potassium and copper deficiencies. Brands include Kelp Help Liquid Kelp Concentrate, Gardens Alive® Liquid Kelp Spray, Bonide® Organic Sea-Green® Kelp Extract Concentrate and Tidal Organics Kelp Meal.

LACEWING

The green lacewing is a very useful beneficial insect. It takes its name from the adult stage, which looks like a small green fly with fine lacy wings. The larval stage looks something like a grub or caterpillar, with an alligator-like mouth making it easy to distinguish from plant-eaters. Both the adult and larval stages are ferocious predators of aphids, whiteflies, small caterpillars, and any other small insects they can catch.

The main drawback to lacewings is that you can't use them with other beneficial insects: the lacewings and their larvae are such fierce predators that will eat other beneficials, or even each other if food is scarce.

Use lacewings in greenhouses and outdoor gardens, but not in grow rooms. Outdoors, the adults will tend to fly away once they emerge from the larval stage.

Main species of interest are *Chrysopa rufilabris* and *Chrysopa carnea*. Buy them as either larvae or eggs from companies such as Bio Ag, Gardens Alive, Rincon-Vitova, Planet Natural, Natural Insect Control and American Insectaries. Plan on using about 1000 eggs or 200 larvae for every 100 square feet (9 square meters).

LADY BEETLES

As cute as lady beetles may be, both the adults and larvae are voracious pest predators. Like lacewings, ladybeetles are also best suited to greenhouse and outdoor gardens. They tend to make suicide dives at the hot lights, and you'll end up with dead insects all over your growspace. Though if you buy them as adults they're even more likely to fly away outdoors.

Choose the species depending on your pest. *Hippodamia convergens* attacks aphids, while *Cryptolaemus montouzieri* and *Ryzobius lophanthae* devour mealybugs and scale. Buy them as adults or larvae from companies such as Bio Ag, Gardens Alive, Rincon-Vitova, Planet Natural, The Ladybug Company, Ladybug Farms and EcoSolutions. Plan on using about 150 adults or larvae for every 100 square feet (9 square meters).

LIME

Lime is a general term for several calcium or calcium-magnesium compounds. All are highly alkaline, and can be used to adjust soil pH upward or to correct calcium and magnesium deficiencies. All of these release calcium/magnesium slowly into the soil.

All forms of lime suitable for gardening can be found in large garden centers and through online garden supply shops. These different varieties of lime include:

- Hydrated lime: Also called slaked lime, this is calcium hydroxide ($Ca(OH)_2$). It is the most alkaline form of lime suitable for gardening, so only small amounts are needed to adjust soil pH. It is widely available, usually under various local or store brands.

- Garden lime: Garden lime is crushed limestone or oyster shells. The main component is calcium carbonate ($CaCO_3$), the same form of calcium found in ordinary eggshells. It is less strongly alkaline than hydrated lime, but still raises soil pH. Brands include Planet Natural Oyster Shell Lime and Espoma® Organic Traditions™ Garden Lime.

- Dolomitic lime: A lime that contains dolomite, a mineral high in magnesium. This makes it useful for treating magnesium as well as calcium deficiencies. Brands include Speedi-Grow® Agricultural Lime and Espoma® Organic Traditions™ Dolomitic Lime, and many others.

- Liquid lime: Liquid lime products are very finely ground garden lime or dolomitic lime in a liquid suspension. Because the particles are so finely divided they raise soil pH more quickly than regular powdered limes do. Brands include Turbo Turf Liquid Lime Plus®, Aggrene Natural Liquid Lime® and Aggrand Organic Liquid Lime®.

LIMONENE

Limonene is refined from the oil of citrus rinds. It has a pleasant citrus odor and is the active ingredient in many new cleaning products. It is a broad-spectrum insecticide effective against ants, aphids, fungus gnats, mealybugs, scales, spider mites and whiteflies. Limonene is the active ingredient in Ortho Home Defense Indoor Insect Killer®, Concern Citrus Home Pest Control®, Clean-Green® All-Purpose Cleaner and in products made by Orange Guard such as D'bug and Enviro-cide.

Limonene also has fungicidal qualities. I've used pure diluted limonene and it controlled powdery mildew, but did not eradicate it. Perhaps I should have used a higher concentration.

MAGNESIUM SULFATE

Magnesium sulfate ($MgSO_4$) is sold in most large drug stores as Epsom salts. It is one of the fastest methods of correcting magnesium and sulfur deficiencies. Apply a solution of 1 teaspoon of Epsom salts per gallon of water (5 mL per 4 Liters) in hydroponic reservoirs or as a foliar spray to treat deficiencies. Use 1 teaspoon per quart of water (5 mL per 1000 mL) in planting mixes. After the first treatment, treat with one-quarter dose with each watering or change of reservoir.

MECHANICAL CONTROLS

Many pests can be effectively controlled by physically removing and destroying them. Often these methods can prevent or eliminate minor infestations, and they supplement other controls in more severe infestations. Some of the more common methods include:

Air filtration: Fungal spores and small insect pests such as aphids, spider mites and whiteflies can enter a growspace through the air intake. A fine dust filter keeps these pests out.

Boiling water: Pour boiling water into anthills to destroy these pests. Do not use this method within about three feet (1 meter) of the plants, however, as it will damage their roots.

Bug zappers: Flying insects such as egg-laying moths are attracted to the blue light and electrocuted on the charged grid.

Handpicking: Slugs, snails, caterpillars, and similar large pests can be picked off the plants by hand whenever they're spotted. Crush them or drop them in a bucket of soapy water to drown them. Look for snails and slugs in the early morning hours, as they hide from light during the day.

Physical barriers: A water moat prevents ants from crossing. For example put plant containers on blocks in a wide pan, and fill the pan with water. Use old vegetable cans as cutworm barriers at the bases of plants. Wrap plants in steel wool to discourage rats. Use copper tape or wire to keep out slugs and snails.

Vacuuming: An ordinary vacuum cleaner can help control whiteflies, spider mites (and their webs), aphids, caterpillars and ants. Use the vacuum hose and brush attachment, or a handheld vacuum cleaner such as a Dustbuster, to suck them out off the plants. Don't get the hose close enough to suck leaves or buds in, as this may damage them.

Water spray: Remove and drown aphids, mites, ants and caterpillars by knocking them off the plants with a strong stream of water from a hose.

Wiping: Remove mealybugs and scale using a cotton swab moistened with rubbing alcohol.

MILK

Milk kills powdery mildew so well that rose growers all over the world have adopted it for their fungicidal sprays. It is used by home gardeners and commercial growers for many other crops as well. Use 1 part milk to 9 parts water. I've only used 1% milk, but some recipes call for either whole or skim milk and use up to 1 part in 5 milk. Some recipes add garlic or cinnamon to the mix. When using more than 30% milk, a benign mold is reported to grow on top of the leaves. This mold is harmless to the plant, but not good for smokers, so if you notice such growth after using a milk spray, just reduce the concentration of milk in subsequent sprays.

Use a milk spray at the first sign of infection. Then protect the new growth weekly.

MINUTE PIRATE BUGS

The minute pirate bug (Orius insidius) is a tiny (about 3 mm long) beneficial insect. They are serious predators, and use their piercing mouths to suck the life out of aphids, mealybugs, scale, and thrips. Buy them as adults from companies such as Planet Natural, Rincon-Vitova, Bioplanet and Natural Insect Control. Plan on using about 50 adults for every 100 square feet (9 square meters).

MYCORRHIZAE

"*Mycorrhizae*" literally means "fungus-roots" and defines the beneficial symbiotic relationship between specialized soil fungi (*Mycorrhizal* fungi) and plant roots. A garden of microbes grows along a plant's root surfaces. *Mycorrhizal* fungi extract nutrients and transport them to the root. There are two types of these beneficial soil fungi: *endomycorrhizae* actually penetrate the plant's root cells, while *ectomycorrhiza* form sheaths at the root tip.

Custom blended mycorrhizal mixes can be added to your soil to encourage healthy root growth. Mycorrhizal products include MycoApply®, Rooters™ Mycorrhizae Super Pack, Plant Success™, MycoGrow™ and SoilMoist™, among others. Benefits include:

- Improved nutrient and water uptake
- Improved root growth

- Improved plant growth and yield
- Reduced transplant shock
- Reduced drought stress

NEEM OIL

Neem oil is pressed from the seed of the neem tree (*Azadirachta indica*), native to Southeast Asia, but now cultivated worldwide. The crude oil has both insecticidal and fungicidal properties, and contains at least 70 components. One group of these is the azadirachtins, which are said to account for 90% of the oil's insecticidal activity. Other compounds including meliantriol, salannin, nimbin and nimbidin also have fungicidal qualities. Neem oil has low mammalian toxicity. In fact it is sometimes used as a toothpaste ingredient in India and neem twigs are chewed and used as toothbrushes. It degrades rapidly once it is applied so it is safe for the environment including non-target species and beneficial insects. It is an effective killer of ants, aphids, fungus gnats, leaf miners, mealybugs, scale, thrips, whiteflies, gray mold, Septoria and powdery mildew.

Neem oil protects plants from fungus in several ways. First it has fungicidal properties on contact as it disrupts the organism's metabolism. Secondly, it forms a barrier between the plant and the invading fungus. Thirdly, it inhibits spore germination. It has translinear action, that is, it is absorbed by the leaf and moves around using the leaf's circulatory system. It can also be used as a systemic. Neem oil products are effective as foliar sprays, and may also be added to soil or grow media in the irrigation water (1 teaspoon neem oil per quart, or 5 mL per liter). When applied in this way neem products are taken up by the plant's roots and distributed throughout the plant. As a foliar spray, Neem oil should be diluted with water and a dash of wetting agent to a 1-2% solution. This solution should be used within 8 hours. The fungicidal and insecticidal effects are more potent when applied by spray, but the systemic neem lasts longer. For fungicidal applications neem oil is best used before the plant or the garden exhibits a major infection. Used in this way, it prevents the spores from germinating.

Azadirachtin and some other components can be removed from the oil with alcohol. The oil that remains after this treatment is called Clarified Hydrophobic Extract of Neem Oil. This gives three main classes of neem garden products:

- Those with azadirachtin act as broad-spectrum insecticides.

Brands include Agroneem, Azatrol, Bioneem and Neemix.

- Those that contain hydrophobic extract of neem oil are both fungicidal and insecticidal, but less effective as insecticides than those based on azadirachtin. Brands include Trilogy; Tri-act and Green Light Fruit, Nut, & Vegetable Spray.

- Those that contain both azadirachtin and extract of neem oil, or pure pressed and filtered neem oil, are more effective as insecticides than either alone. Brands include Azatin-Plus, Dyna-gro™ and Ecoside.

Neem oil should be applied for 3 weeks before harvesting.

NITRATE SALTS

Nitrate (NO_3) is the form of nitrogen most readily available to plants. Many nitrate salts, such as calcium nitrate ($Ca(NO_3)_2$) and potassium nitrate (KNO_3), provide a quick shot of soluble nitrogen for treating nitrogen deficiencies. Brands include Champion, SQM Hydroponica and Ultrasol.

PARASITOID WASPS

Several different species of wasp act as parasites on garden pests. These wasps are non-social, stingless to humans, and so tiny that once you release them you may never see them again. The entire life-cycle of parasitoid wasps revolves around the host pests. They lay their eggs in eggs, larvae, or adult pests (depending on species), and the larval wasp then consumes the pest from within. Adult wasps often eat pests as well, depending on the species.

Choose the species depending on your pest. Encarsia species attack whiteflies. *Trichogramma* species go after caterpillars. Aphidius and Aphelinus species destroy aphids. Choose *Dacnusa, Diglyphus* and *Opius* species for leafminers. *Leptomastix, Anagyrus* and *Metaphycus* parasitize mealybugs and scale. Buy them as pupae from companies such as Buglogical, Hydro-Gardens, IPM Labs, Natural Insect Control, Planet Natural and Rincon-Vitova. Plan on using about 100 pupae for every 100 square feet (9 square meters). Some pests may require multiple applications for full control.

pH UP AND pH DOWN

pH-Up and pH Down are generic terms for alkaline and acid pH adjustors, respectively. They are used to adjust water pH in indoor gardens, and may come as either a powder or liquid. The active ingredient is usually potassium hydroxide (KOH) or potash (K_2CO_3) for pH-Up, or phosphoric acid (H_3PO_4) in pH-Down. Brands include General Hydroponics, GroWell, and Growth Technology.

Most fungi can grow only within a certain pH range. An alkaline solution with a pH of 8 makes the environment inhospitable for the fungus and stops its growth. Making up such a solution with pH-Down and applying it as a foliar spray is one of the simplest means of controlling foliar fungi such as gray mold and powdery mildew. It can be used on critically infected plants.

POTASSIUM BICARBONATE

Potassium bicarbonate ($KHCO_3$) is used in the food industry but is also useful as a fungicide against gray mold, Fusarium, powdery mildew and Septoria leaf spot. It is a wettable powder that raises the pH of the environment surrounding the fungi. Potassium bicarbonate is better than sodium bicarbonate (baking soda) because potassium is one of the macro-nutrients used by plants. It can be used to cure bad infections and used weekly prevents new ones. Potassium bicarbonate is also useful against potassium deficiencies.

Studies show that potassium bicarbonate is more effective as a fungicide when used with an oil and a wetting agent. Use one teaspoon (5 mL) of potassium bicarbonate, a teaspoon of oil and a small amount of wetting agent in a pint (500 mL) of water, or 3 tablespoons (45 mL) each potassium bicarbonate and oil and a half teaspoon of wetting agent in a gallon (3.8 Liters) of water. It is also available commercially in Zero Tolerance® fungicide, Armicarb100®, Kaligreen®, FirstStep®, Remedy®, Milstop®, and other brands. Spray weekly as needed.

POTASSIUM SALTS

Potassium sulfate (K_2SO_4), potassium silicate (K_2SiO_3) and potassium phosphate (K_3PO_4) are highly soluble salts that can be used to supplement a plant's potassium needs without introducing nitrogen (or phosphorous, in the case of the sulfate and silicate). Potassium sulfate is also sometimes called SOP (sulfate of potash). Look for brands such as Champion, Pro-Tekt, Hydro-Gardens, Planet Natural and Allganic™ Potassium.

PREDATOR URINE

Deer avoid areas that smell of predators such as coyotes. Repellents eaters. Stale, strong urine is most effective.

Rather than applying these repellents directly to marijuana plants, create a barrier by applying them to other plants that grow around your garden. Another method is to string a rope or cord around the garden and tie cloth strips to the cord every 3 feet. Apply the repellent to the cloth strips to deter deer. Look for these repellents under brands such as CoyotePee® and Deer Busters® Coyote Urine.

PREDATORY MITES

Set a mite to catch a mite. Predatory mites breed rapidly (especially indoors), and eat fungus gnats, spider mites and thrips. Look for species such *Amblyseius, Galendromus, Hypoaspis, Neoseiulus* and *Phytoseiulus.*

Buy them as adults from companies such as Buglogical, Planet Natural, Hydro-Gardens, Natural Insect Control, Peaceful Valley and EcoSolutions. Plan on using about 30 to 50 adults per plant, or 300 per 100 square feet (9 square meters). Note that while predator mites do reproduce quickly, they can't play catch-up with a rampant spider mite infestation. If your infestation is already out of control then use a non-persistent control to reduce the spider mite population before releasing predator mites.

PREDATORY NEMATODES

These are microscopic creatures that live in soil, and attack pests that spend their larval stages in soil, such as thrips and fungus gnats. Look for species such *Steinernema* and *Heterorhabditis.* They can live for months in soil, so they can be applied as a preventive as well as to control existing infestations.

Unlike many beneficials, predatory nematodes are bought in bulk either as spray solutions or in sponges that you soak in water, then apply the water as a spray or soil drench. There are name brands such as NemaShield™ and Scanmask. Buy from companies such as Buglogical, Planet Natural, Worm's Way, Hydro-Gardens, Natural Insect Control and Peaceful Valley. Coverage rates vary, so apply according to the manufacturer's directions.

PSEUDOMONAS

This is a bacterial genus that contains several fungicidal species. Pseudomonas products such as BioReleaf®, Blight-Ban® and Bac-Pack® control fungi such as Pythium, Fusarium, and gray mold.

Pseudomonas products such as BioReleaf®, Blight-Ban® and Bac-Pack® control fungi such as Pythium, Fusarium, and gray mold. Note that different Pseudomonas species are effective against different pathogens, so check the label to make sure that the one you're buying controls the diseases you're targeting.

PUTRESCENT EGGS

In combination with garlic and capsaicin, rotten eggs are a potent deer repellent. Look for brands such as Deer-Off®. Apply as recommended by the manufacturer.

PYRETHRUM

Pyrethrum is a broad-spectrum natural insecticide, derived from a plant in the chrysanthemum family. It acts on contact, and so must be sprayed directly on the target pests. It is effective against ants, aphids, caterpillars, fungus gnats, leaf miners, mealybugs, scale, spider mites, thrips and whiteflies. Note that pyrethrum is also toxic to many beneficial insects, fish and reptiles.

Pyrethrum formulations range from powders to sprays and are available under many different brand names, including Safer Yard and Garden Insect Spray, Planet Natural® Pyrethrum Powder and PyGanic Crop Protection.

QUATERNARY AMINES

This a class of compounds that act as broad-spectrum disinfectants. They are effective against many algae and many fungal pathogens, including gray mold, Fusarium and Pythium. Use these products for general disinfection of tools and hard surfaces, but do not use them directly on or around edible (or smokeable) plants. Physan 20® and Prontech® are popular quaternary amine preparations for horticultural use.

ROCK PHOSPHATE

Rock phosphate is a naturally occurring phosphate mineral. Used as a soil amendment, it releases phosphorous slowly and helps to prevent phosphorous deficiency. It is available in garden centers under brands such as Montana Natural, Peace of Mind and Espoma Organic Traditions.

Be careful to distinguish between rock phosphate and so-called "superphosphate" or "triple phosphate." Rock phosphate is suitable for organic gardening, but the other two are prepared by treating rock phosphate with powerful acids to make a product that release phosphorous much more quickly. Rock phosphate that has been processed in this way is no longer acceptable in organic gardens. It may release phosphorous too quickly for sustained vegetative growth.

ROTENONE

Rotenone is one of the more toxic natural insecticides. It is a broad-spectrum insecticide, but is also toxic to fish, small amphibians, and even mammals to a lesser degree. It acts by disrupting metabolism at the cellular level. Rotenone will kill most chewing insects (including beneficials), but since there are less-toxic alternatives for most pests it is recommended mainly for insects that resist other insecticides and for very severe infestations that other products have failed to control. It breaks down quickly in air, so plants treated with it are still safe for consumption.

Rotenone is available in many different brands (sometimes in combination with pyrethrum), including Bonide® Rotenone & Pyrethrin Spray, Soilserv® Rotenone-Pyrethrum Spray and Gordon's Garden Guard. Check the label on any rotenone product, as it is often combined with other materials that may or may not be safe for consumption. For example a broad line of "all purpose garden dusts" contains rotenone and copper salts (as a fungicide). The rotenone breaks down harmlessly, but leaves and buds treated with copper should not be consumed.

SACCHAROPOLYSPORA SPINOSA (BENEFICIAL BACTERIA)

This is a soil-dwelling bacterium that produces a powerful insecticidal toxin. The toxin is sold under the brand name Spinosad®, and is an important active ingredient in many garden insecticides. It must be eaten to be effective, and so is useful against ants, caterpillars, leaf miners, spider mites and thrips. It is toxic to bees, however, so use it with caution around flowering plants. Look for it in brands such as Dow Conserve® SC, Entrust®, and Green Light Spinosad.

SESAME OIL

The oil pressed from sesame seeds has both insecticidal and fungicidal properties. It is effective against aphids, fungus gnats, leaf miners, mealybugs, scales, spider mites, thrips, whiteflies, gray mold, Septoria and powdery mildew. It is available under brand names such as Organocide® (a blend of sesame oil and fish oil) and

Green Light® Bioganic® Home and Garden (a mixture of sesame, clove, thyme, soybean and wintergreen oils). You can also make your own using sesame oil from a health food or gourmet shop. Mix it 1% (1 teaspoon per pint or 5 mL per 500mL) with water and a small amount of lecithin and a wetting agent.

SILICA AND SILICATE SALTS

Silica is not known to be essential for plant growth. However, when it is available to them, plants absorb it through their roots. The plants park the silica in the cell wall as well as internally in the cell. They also use it to form protective sheaths near the leaf surface.

Farmers used to protect plants from fungal diseases using sprays made from extracts of plants with high silica content such as the horsetail plant (*Equisetum arvense*), which contains 15 to 40 percent natural silica. In controlled experiments plants with high silica content were protected against powdery mildew. Silica is alkaline so one of its modes of action may be to create a no-grow environment for the fungus.

Plants grown with ample amounts of soluble silica grow thicker cell walls, which results in stronger stems. It helps resist fungal and insect attacks. It also affects the plants sensitivity to absorption and translocation of several macro- and micronutrients. It acts as a "toughening agent," increasing the plant's ability to survive stressful situations such as drought, high salinity and nutrient imbalance.

Hydroponically grown plants with soluble silicon added to the water solution had reduced incidence and severity of powdery mildew in several trials. They also had increased yields and produced thicker, whiter, healthier root systems. Foliar silicon sprays also protect against powdery mildew.

Dyna-Gro Pro-Tekt® is a potassium silicate solution that can be used in soil, hydroponics and foliar applications. Other sources of silica include:

- Pyrophyllite clay is aluminum silicate in powder form. It can be applied as a dust or foliar spray, and is available under a number of brand names (Seaclay, Mineral Magic, Pyroclay).

- Silica stone is a hydroponic medium used in place of clay pellets.

- Greensand is a popular soil and planting mix conditioner that can be used to supplement silica in soils.

- Vermiculite and perlite can be purchased in bulk at garden centers for use in potting soils. They are made from mica, which has a high silica content.

- EcoSand, Clino-Lite and ZeoPro are brands of zeolite mined from volcanic sites. They are composed of aluminum silicates, as well as potassium, calcium, magnesium, iron and traces of manganese and tin.

- Diatomaceous earth is made from the shells of tiny marine organisms that are very high in silica.

SILVER

Colloidal silver is a suspension of very fine silver particles. It has a long history as a general purpose disinfectant, including use as an algaecide in pools and hydroponic systems. Used according to label directions, it will not harm marijuana plants. Several commercial brands are available, including Regal Pool Chemicals Silver Algaecide, Haviland Silver Algaecide and Silver Algaedyne®.

SOAPS

Insecticidal soaps are mild soap solutions that damage the exoskeletons of soft-bodied insects (such as aphids, whiteflies, mealybugs, scales, spider mites and thrips) and cause them to dehydrate. They work by direct contact, and so must be sprayed directly on the target pest.

You can make your own pesticidal soap solutions by mixing a few drops of a mild soap (the author prefers Dr. Bronner's Peppermint® castile soap) in a pint of water. However some soaps can be toxic to plants, so always test a new soap by spraying it on a small area of one plant and waiting a day or two to check for damage. Commercial insecticidal soaps such as Neudorff's Insecticidal Soap, Concern Insect Killing Soap, Monterey Quick, Safer Insecticidal Soap and M-Pede® have been pre-tested to ensure that they will not harm plants. Soaps are also sold as algaecides under brands such as Schultz Garden Safe® Moss and Algae Killer and DeMoss®.

SODIUM BICARBONATE

Sodium bicarbonate ($NaHCO_3$), baking soda, has the same mode of action as potassium bicarbonate and is effective against the same diseases. It is often used by gardeners instead of potassium bicarbonate because it is readily available in most kitchens. However, it is not as effective as potassium bicarbonate and leaves sodium in the soil when it breaks down. Although I haven't heard of any cases where there was so much sodium build-up that it affected plant growth, it is prudent to use potassium bicarbonate.

There is no problem with using baking soda at the first sight of powdery mildew. It works and has been used by finicky rose growers for more than 70 years. Use one teaspoon (5 mL) of potassium bicarbonate, a teaspoon of oil and a few drops of wetting agent or castile soap in a pint of water (500mL), or 3 tablespoons (40 mL) each potassium bicarbonate and oil and a wetting agent or ½ teaspoon liquid castile soap in a gallon of water (3.8 L). Spray weekly.

STREPTOMYCES GRISEOVIRIDIS (BENEFICIAL BACTERIA)

These bacteria produce fungicidal agents effective against Fusarium, gray mold, and Pythium. Brands such as MycoStop®, RootGuard®, and Microgrow® contain Streptomyces formulations. These products are usually applied as a soil drench before symptoms appear.

SULFUR

Sulfur has been used to control Septoria, gray mold and powdery mildew for centuries. Several foliar sprays containing sulfur are available, such as Thiocal® and Safer® Defender Fungicide, but they may cause leaf damage. Check such products on a few branches and wait a day or two to check for problems before applying to your entire garden. The preferred delivery method for most marijuana growers is vaporization. Sulfur vaporizers use powdered elemental sulfur (also called garden sulfur), such as Thiolux Jet or Yellowstone Brand Hi-Purity Prill, heated in a container above a 60-watt light bulb. The vapors condense into a fine film of very low pH sulfur granules on the leaf surfaces. The low pH environment inhibits fungal growth. Sulfur candles are available at some garden centers and work in a similar way.

Note that sulfur vaporizers produce a strong smell of sulfur. Air out your growspace after using a sulfur vaporizer. Sulfur should not be used with oils or when the temperature is over 85º F (29º C).

In addition to its fungicidal properties, garden sulfur is useful for lowering the pH of alkaline soils, and for correcting sulfur deficiencies.

TRICHODERMA (BENEFICIAL FUNGI)

Several trichoderma species, such as *T. harzianum*, provide protection against fungal diseases including gray mold, Septoria, Fusarium, Verticillium and Pythium. PlantShield® and RootShield® use a particularly effective patented strain of *T. harzianum*: strain KRL-AG2, developed at Cornell University. Look for other brands also such as Trichodex®, Bio-Fungus® and BioTrek®. These products are applied as a soil drench for Fusarium, Verticillium and Pythium, or as a foliar spray for gray mold and Septoria.

UREA

Urea is not an organic fertilizer, but it is one of the best relatively available nitrogen sources. Because urea is so high in nitrogen (NPK 45-0-0), follow the label directions carefully to avoid nutrient burn. Brands include Espoma Quick Solutions Urea and many local and store brands.

UVC LIGHT

Special ultraviolet lamps are available under names like Big Blue®, Turbo Twist®, and Air Probe Sanitizer™. Place these lamps in hydroponic systems and the ventilation systems of growrooms, where their light helps to eliminate mold spores (such as powdery mildew and Pythium), algae, and other pathogens. Note that a UVC lamp in a hydro system will eliminate all microorganisms in the water, including beneficial microbes if you have introduced them.

VINEGAR

Vinegar is toxic to powdery mildew. Use it at the rate of 1 tablespoon per quart (15 mL per Liter) of water. Some gardeners recommend alternating vinegar with potassium bicarbonate and milk.

WETTING AGENTS

This is a broad class of compounds that break the surface tension of water. This prevents water solutions from beading up on plant surfaces and helps them penetrate into soil. Castile soap (the author prefers Dr. Bronner's Peppermint®) can be used as a wetting agent. Commercial brands for organic gardening include Coco-Wet, ThermX™ 70®, Phyto Plus® Foliar Friend™, Natural Wet® and RainGrow Superflow™.

ZINC PHOSPHIDE

Zinc phosphide (Zn_3P_2) is an old rat poison now seeing a resurgence in popularity. It is fast acting, and more specific than some other poisons because it has a strong garlic odor that attracts rodents but repels most other animals. It is sold in baits under brands such as Nu-Kil®, Eraze™ Rodent Pellets, Prozap® Zinc Phosphide Oat Bait and ZP Rodent Bait AG. As with all rat poisons, zinc phosphide baits should be deployed in tamper-proof bait stations in accordance with the manufacturer's instructions.

ZINC SALTS

Zinc sulfate ($ZnSO_4$) and zinc oxide (ZnO) provide supplemental zinc in cases of zinc deficiency. Brands include Spectrum Chemical, BLU-MIN® Liquid Zinc Sulfate and NutraSul Plus 18% Zinc–Sulfur Fertilizer. It is also available in combination with Fe and Mn.

CHART OF CONTROLS

Problem	Control
Ants	Ant Baits, Barriers, Boiling Water, Boric Acid, Capsaicin, Carbon Dioxide, Cinnamon Oil, Clove Oil, Cream of Tartar, Diatomaceous Earth, Garlic, Limonene, Neem Oil, Pyrethrum, *Saccharopolyspora spinosa*, Vacuuming, Water Spray
Algae	Barley Straw Rafts, Grapefruit Seed Extract, Hydrogen Peroxide, Silver, UVC light, Soap
Aphids	Air Intake Filters, Aphid midge, *Beauveria bassiana*, Capsaicin, Carbon Dioxide, Cinnamon Oil, Clove Oil, Coriander Oil, Garlic, Horticultural Oil, Insecticidal Soap, Lacewing, Lady Beetle, Limonene, Minute Pirate Bug, Neem Oil, Parasitoid Wasps (Aphidius and Aphelinus species), Pyrethrum, Vacuuming, Water Spray
Boron Deficiency	Boric Acid, Compost and Compost Tea
Calcium Deficiency	Cal-Mag Fertilizers, Calcium Nitrate, Dolomitic Lime, Garden Lime, Gypsum
Caterpillars	*Bacillus thuringiensis,* Barriers, Bug zappers, Garlic, Handpicking, Insecticidal Soaps, Neem Oil, Parasitoid Wasps (Trichogramma species), Pyrethrum, Rotenone, *Saccharopolyspora spinosa,* Vacuuming, Water Spray
Copper Deficiency	Chelated Copper, Compost and Compost Tea, Copper Fungicides, Greensand, Hydroponic Micronutrient Products, Kelp Concentrates
Damping Off	*Bacillus subtilis,* Clove oil, Copper, Compost and Compost Tea, Coriander oil, Gliocladium, Pseudomonas, Quaternary amines, Sesame oil, *Streptomyces griseoviridis,* Trichoderma
Deer	Capsaicin, Fences, Garlic, Predator Urine, Putrescent Eggs
Fungus Gnat	*Bacillus thuringiensis,* Barriers (sand, cloth, cardboard, etc.), Cinnamon Oil and Tea, Diatomaceous Earth, Horticultural Oil, Insecticidal Soaps, Neem Oil, Predatory Mites, Predatory Nematodes, Pyrethrum
Fusarium	*Bacillus pumilus, Bacillus subtilis,* Compost and Compost Tea, Gliocladium, Mycorrhizae, *Streptomyces griseoviridis*

Problem	Control
Gophers	Capsaicin, Carbon Dioxide, Castor Oil, Fumigants, Traps
Gray Mold	*Bacillus pumilus, Bacillus subtilis,* Clove Oil, Compost and Compost Tea, Copper, Coriander Oil, Humidity Control, Neem Oil, pH Up, Potassium Bicarbonate, Pseudomonas, Quaternary Amines, Sesame Oil, Sodium Bicarbonate, Sulfur, *Trichoderma*
Iron Deficiency	Chelated Iron, Compost and Compost Tea, Chelated Iron, Hydroponic Micronutrient Products, Iron Salts (Sulfates and Oxides), Rusty Water
Leaf Miners	*Beauveria bassiana,* Capsaicin, Horticultural Oil, Neem Oil, Parasitoid Wasps (Dacnusa, Diglyphus and Opius species), Pyrethrum, *Saccharopolyspora spinosa*
Leaf Septoria	*Bacillus pumilus,* Cinnamon Oil, Clove Oil, Compost and Compost Tea, Copper, Coriander Oil, Neem Oil, pH Up, Potassium Bicarbonate, Sesame Oil, Sodium Bicarbonate, Sulfur, *Trichoderma*
Magnesium Deficiency	Cal-Mag Fertilizers, Compost and Compost Tea, Dolomitic Lime, Magnesium Sulfate
Manganese Deficiency	Chelated Manganese, Compost and Compost Tea, Greensand, Hydroponic Micronutrient Products, Fe-Zn-Mn Fertilizer
Mealybugs and Scale	Alcohol Wipes, Cinnamon Oil, Clove Oil, Horticultural Oil, Insecticidal Soaps, Lacewings, Lady Beetles, Limonene, Minute Pirate Bug, Neem Oil, Parasitoid Wasps (Leptomastix, Anagyrus and Metaphycus species), Pyrethrum
Moles	Capsaicin, Carbon Dioxide, Castor Oil
Molybdenum Deficiency	Hydroponic Micronutrient Products, Molybdenum Supplements
Nitrogen Deficiency	Alfalfa Meal, Cottonseed Meal, Fish Emulsion and Fish Meal, High-Nitrogen Fertilizers, High-Nitrogen Guano, Nitrate Salts, Urea
Phosphorous Deficiency	Greensand, High-Phosphorous Fertilizers, High-Phosphorous Guano, Rock Phosphate
Potassium Deficiency	Granite Dust, Greensand, High-Potassium Fertilizers, Kelp Concentrates, Potassium Salts, Wood Ashes

Problem	Control
Powdery Mildew	*Ampelomyces quisqualis,* Vinegar, *Bacillus pumilis, Bacillus subtilis,* Cinnamon Oil, Compost and Compost Tea, Copper, Coriander Oil, Garlic, Hydrogen Peroxide, Limonene, Milk, Neem Oil, pH-Up, Potassium Bicarbonate, Sesame Oil, Sodium Bicarbonate, Sulfur
Pythium	*Bacillus subtilis,* Clove oil, Compost and Compost Tea, Copper, Coriander oil, *Gliocladium,* Pseudomonas, Quaternary amines, Sesame oil, *Streptomyces griseoviridis, Trichoderma*
Rats	Barriers, Cats, Cholecalciferol, Traps, Zinc Phosphide
Silicon Deficiency	Diatomaceous Earth, Silica and Silicate Salts
Slugs and Snails	Copper Tape, Diatomaceous Earth, Handpicking, Iron Phosphate
Spider Mites	Air Intake Filters, *Beauveria bassiana,* Capsaicin, Carbon Dioxide, Cinnamon Oil, Clove Oil, Coriander Oil, Garlic, Horticultural Oil, Insecticidal Soap, Lady Beetles, Limonene, Minute Pirate Bugs, Neem Oil, Predatory Mites, Pyrethrum, *Saccharopolyspora spinosa,* Sesame Oil, Vacuuming, Water Spray
Sulfur Deficiency	Magnesium Sulfate, Gypsum, Sulfur Powder
Thrips	*Beauveria bassiana,* Capsaicin, Carbon dioxide, Cinnamon Oil, Clove Oil, Coriander Oil, Horticultural Oil, Insecticidal Soap, Minute Pirate Bugs, Neem Oil, Predatory Mites, Predatory Nematodes, Pyrethrum, *Saccharopolyspora spinosa*
Verticillium Wilt	*Bacillus subtilis,* Compost and Compost Tea, *Trichoderma*
Whiteflies	Air Intake Filters, *Beauveria bassiana,* Capsaicin, Carbon Dioxide, Cinnamon Oil, Clove Oil, Coriander Oil, Garlic, Horticultural Oil, Insecticidal Soap, Lacewings, Limonene, Minute Pirate Bugs, Neem Oil, Parasitoid Wasps (Encarsia species), Pyrethrum, Sesame Oil, Vacuuming
Zinc Deficiency	Chelated Zinc, Hydroponic Micronutrient Products, Fe-Zn-Mn Fertilizer, Zinc Salts